The Indie Author's Bible:

A DIY guide to start right, what to do once you're in print, and beyond

The Indie Author's Bible:

A DIY guide to start right, what to do once you're in print, and beyond

by

Christopher D Schmitz

ISBN: 978-1-63227-205-8
BISAC REF015000 Reference / Personal & Practical Guides

PUBLISHED BY CHRISTOPHER D SCHMITZ
please visit:
http://www.authorchristopherdschmitz.com

For my wife, who puts up with me sometimes, kinda—sorta… and the endless hours I force her to act like my beta reader.

Table of Contents

Going Traditional

Self-Publishing your Book

Now that your book is Available

Bookstores, signings, conventions, pitching, Etc.

Other fun & no-so fun Information

Foreword

Why did I write this book?

You've probably seen a boatload of articles and blogs talking about how XYZ sold 9,000 copies in one week, or how ZYX topped a bestseller list, or how YXZ gained a gazillion email and twitter followers with one simple, "must see to believe," sure-fire formula.

Here's why I'm writing this book: all of that is crap. Those "magic bullets" or "special classes" or course materials validated by seemingly impressive credentials are mostly junk meant to get you to click a link or surrender your email address. Don't they work? Maybe… but like less than 1% of the time. Getting repeatedly burned by empty promises proves very disheartening; it's easy to think that somehow *you* failed to make the "quick and easy/can't lose tactic" succeed. Those promoted methods are nearly always written by the exception, rather than the rule. *This book* is written by a real indie author. One who made lots of mistakes. One who tried a bunch of those special programs and newsletters. One whose journey is probably a lot like yours has been/will be.

A few years back I learned to play the bagpipes and went in search of my first set to purchase (I'll reference piping a few times as it taught me many life lessons). I came across many teachers offering advice. One piece stuck with me about the "quick and easy path." A low-cost set of quality bagpipes is about a thousand bucks. If you hop onto eBay or Amazon you will see numerous listings ranging from $100-$200. Those are what we call Paki-pipes (made by low-cost imitators in Pakistan and surrounding regions.) They don't quite work right. I have a pair that I got for free after learning to play properly and players with proper skills can make them sound *close* to how they should... this teacher, however, stated, "in the decades I've been teaching, no student that ever tried to learn on a set of Paki Pipes stayed with it. They each became frustrated and quit because the things would never work and sound right."

Those pipers quit on a dream because their frustration outgrew their passion. Don't buy into the idea that the "exception" is the norm—that's some guy selling Paki Pipes. Look for the rule rather than the exception and know that big success requires sacrifice, effort, and proper investment.

This book is mostly a chronicle of things that I've tried and learned as I bumbled my way through the writing indiesphere and achieved some modicum of success, at least by my own metric (and as an Indie, that's the one that matters.) It's written honestly and sometimes tongue in cheek.

I write. A lot. I still have a day job. I still get super excited when a stranger tells me that they read my book. I make a few bucks selling books—but I also get to meet lots of interesting people. Hopefully your journey gets to be the same—or even better.

Fair warning, I'm not an actual expert... just a guy who learned a few things from early mistakes. Maybe I can keep you from stepping on those same turds I did along your way.

--Christopher D Schmitz

Introduction

I meet lots of people when I do book signings. Other writers often come up to me, excited to announce, "I'm writing a book, too!" I honestly believe that everyone has a story. You do too, whether you plan to write it or not, you have a story and it matters.

People tend to just jump in and learn as they go, writers especially. Born story-tellers tend to let their worlds unfold as they unveil and fulfill the story by putting it down on paper... the story might have been murky until putting it in print made it clear for the first time.

A first-time author's approach to the publishing world is often like that and that's not usually a good thing: we often forage through the dark on our own. The indie world is a jungle and there are few well-beaten paths—but unlike you'd expect, even some of those well-beaten paths end in spike pits, too. Many predators have figured out how to lay clever traps like that (so-called author-services and disguised vanity presses). The best bet is to never travel alone (network) and seek guidance from others (like this book.)

Some of us made it out of the jungle alive, but many fall into dangerous pits that we can't get out of. I fell into a few holes early on and managed to crawl out—that's why I decided to do things better: to seek advice from others.

Years ago, when I finally decided to tackle the huge challenge of learning the great highland bagpipes I looked for info on learning as a self-taught musician. Everywhere I looked pipers pleaded for newbies to get lessons instead because of the unique difficulties of the instrument. I heeded their advice and weekly drove 150 miles (one way) to take a lesson from an instructor. Doing things right requires a level of commitment beyond simple desire or the ability to fly by the seat of your pants. Some things in life are less forgiving than others. Like piping, the writing world is one of those kinds of things.

I'm not vain enough to think that I can truly be your end-all resource and answer every question, but I can certainly tell you how I tried, failed, figured things out, and found what works for me. If I can set you on the right path, sometimes that's all a person needs!

Mostly this book grew out of articles I've written and posted on my blog, so this book will continue growing through new editions as I learn more and fail more. You should definitely follow my blog, in addition to those others that I cite, and the links in the back matter. The collective wisdom shared by authors I follow is indispensable.

You can find me at Inside the Inkwell:
https://wordpress.com/post/authorchristopherdschmitz.wordpress.com

Quick start Guide.
A (Kind-of) Sequential Roadmap to Getting Your Book Into Print Now (for no money)

I have the privilege of meeting lots of young/up and coming writers when I do booths at conventions. They sometimes look at my table with its stacks of paperbacks bearing my name and ask with wide eyes, "You did all this?"

It's a perfect open door for me to share with authors about the form, craft, nuts and bolts, etc. of writing. It's a big world, and so there is no sense getting bent out of shape or jealous when another writer wants to break in. Wishing for others to fail (even secretly) is never a strategy for success. I've tried to be as much of an encourager and guide as possible to other authors (even giving criticism when needed.)

One thing often asked by those wide-eyed writers is, "How?" Holding a paperback in your hand requires many steps in order to make it a reality, and so I've created a handy-dandy roadmap for those with fierce DIY inclinations. The best part is that this checklist/guide is a potentially FREE route to getting your book in print, available for purchase in all 3 major formats, and on bookstore shelves (provided you have the network/skills to get art and editing done without a cost.)

Upfront I want to tell you something I repeatedly tell people who asks me about indie writing/self-publishing: "If someone's trying to sell you a 'publishing package,' run away. It's either a scam or they're making money off of authors, not books." I write more about this later, but keep an eye out and I guarantee you will find sharks in your swimming pool.

1. write book

2. edit book to high quality and properly format
3. secure cover art
4. write back cover text including bio
5. decide on book pricing
6. upload all files to Createspace and Ingramspark and publish on Createspace
7. push novel to Kindle for eBook version
8. add bio to Amazon author profile
9. put book into distribution through both Createspace's channels and mirror at Ingramspark (search for and utilize an Ingram coupon code to avoid fees. I've never been able to *not* find a code,) to make books available to brick and mortar stores
10. mirror eBook version to Smashwords so that it is pushed to all major retailers (iTunes, BN, kobo, etc.)
11. partner with an Indie producer on ACX and have book converted to Audible/audio
12. work to build a platform (social media, website, and email campaign service).
13. begin adverts utilizing Amazon associates

Of course, this roadmap is only really relevant if you have already decided to go the independent publishing route, as many people do. Even many traditional authors (including well-known ones) choose to engage in both sides of the business, letting publishing houses handle much of their work, but also dabbling with some Indie/self-pub stuff, too. For writers making a serious living on their efforts, the Indie route provides a bunch of features and freedoms that make it highly lucrative because of their publishing strategy.

There are many ways to hit all the points on the list that meet your vision for your book, and the order doesn't *need* to be followed in a truly linear fashion (I often do steps 3 and 4 during my 3rd draft, for example… it keeps me inspired, but for some it tempts them to launch their book too soon.)

If you choose to follow these 13 steps, you should have all the major pieces in place to begin your journey as an Indie. From here, the only one who can stop you from succeeding is *you!* Don't wax apathetic or release the book into the wild and "hope for the best." You've got to keep a steady hand on it, but you've got this.

You're an author, so do author stuff!

Writers Write... But They Are Readers First!

Read! Be a consumer of what you sell—this applies to all aspects of life: know your market, at least know what others are doing. For writer's it means reading... not just writing.

As a musician, I got a great piece of advice from a newsletter I subscribe to. The company that runs it is dedicated to selling classes to help you become a better instrumentalist. Their advice was so simple I couldn't believe I'd overlooked it: listen to other players—know what good quality sounds like. I started listening to other soloists and listened to how certain things *ought* to sound—especially for tunes I also played. I learned a few tricks, reinforced good techniques, and began to notice some weak areas to work on. If I only ever listened to myself, I would never improve. It's the same with every aspect of life—it's why industry leading companies hire consultants... we need to get out of our own heads sometimes. We need to see quality so we can aim for a higher mark.

In bands, in the professional world, in the writing sphere, across the board, I've encountered others who believe themselves at the top of their game and refuse to examine what others do because they are too busy "doing it their own way." Over the years I've noticed bands that succeed are willing to look at other groups that had success and find ways to emulate the successful traits. Bands that fail usually claim to be great and laugh off any advice (of course they aren't "signed" yet and have an excuse for that.) The reason for this is fear. Taking advice means self-examination and admitting that their ego doesn't match reality.

Don't be afraid of self-comparison. It is a good thing to have a standard you are trying to achieve. If you are afraid because you won't meet "market standards," then you probably should have spent some time on another draft, paid for an editor, rerecorded that track in the studio, instituted some changes at work to improve yourself, or waited to release your product.

Know what's out there. Read. Keep an open mind. If you "don't have time," then get creative. I've been reading by listening to books on Audible while driving or exercising. If you are dedicated to excellence you will find ways to hone your craft.

I mentioned in the intro that everyone has a story—that's part of the human condition. When you meet people at conventions and book signings you *will* meet other people who want to tell you about the book that *they* are working on. Their project may or may not ever reach a conclusion; it might not even be a real endeavor, but people like to talk and find ways to co connect. I wish I was kidding, but I actually had a man tell me *he was writing the best book ever*. When I asked what he liked to read (mainly to connect to stories that interested him,) he stated, "oh, I don't read. Nothing out there really interests me. That's why I'm going to write this book as soon as I find time."

Normally I'm polite but I actually told this guy that he had no business writing a book if he hadn't read one since being forced in junior high lit class. "That's a little like predicting you could win a Nascar race when all your driving experience is limited to Mario Cart."

All great writers are readers first. Crack a book. I'll even provide recommendations.

How To Start

A lady stood at my convention table and said, "I've always wanted to write a book. Let me ask you this, how do you even start?"

I confess, I didn't know how to answer her at first. I probably said something nice to encourage her, but likely bumbled my way through an actual answer. Once something comes naturally to you, you tend to forget all of the little steps that brought you there. Can you remember what it was like before you knew how to read, or ride a bicycle, or transfer public transportation lines? It may be scary the first few times and then you forget what even *that* was like.

Busses scare me. I see little kids in the city hop from bus to bus. It takes me twenty minutes of reading brochures to hesitantly hop onto a connecting stop—not because I am unable, but because I have no idea what I'm doing. I grew up in the country where everyone had a car—public transit wasn't even a thought for us. *I didn't know where to begin.* Writing is like that for some people, and everyone's starting process is somewhat different. Some people are meticulous outliners, some people use notecards (yes, like in high school), and some people are "pantsers" (people who sit and write by the "seat of their pants.")

Since there is no hard and fast rule, what I *can* tell you is how I used to write and how I write, now.

I used to be a pantser. As I got better at writing—and thus more meticulous in my editing, I became an outliner by accident. It happened organically. My old process was that I would write my thoughts, collecting each general chapter's worth of thoughts in a page(s) in a notebook: what the major events of the plot were and things that needed to happen and then I'd jot subplot info in the margins. After the story was complete I would actually go back and write an outline off of that—mainly for editing purpose as I would sometimes check for continuity errors or just need to know where to go in order to make a change I decided on later. *Now, that's how I write, but I outline first.* I'm doing the same thing, only digitally instead of on paper. I also keep pages and pages of other thoughts, character notes, etc. I usually consult it several times per edit and high light things that I've missed or need to pay attention to during the next draft.

Because I start with an outline (that I update as I write) editing has become easier for me. But that still doesn't say *how* I start. I just do.

When I look at my outline, I don't see tiny parts, I see the story as a whole—it's good to mentally revisit what you want to accomplish with the story regularly. Then I zero in on *what I want to write today*. I look at that part on my outline and then I sit down to write it (it helps to have a regular space, make sure your calendar isn't crammed with other stuff, turn off social media, have something to drink nearby; allow yourself to engage in the story. Once you are in the swing of things, you may find you want to use all your scraps of free time to write, too. I hate to put things down once I've begun them and I began saving things in the cloud so I could take a story with to work on it in the five or ten minutes before a meeting or event. Even if I only write two sentences, it's progress. Just be sure to set aside some of that time to dedicate to writing.

Progress may come slow at first. It might read like trash—that's okay. Just get it on paper. Sometimes you just need to start in order to prime the pump and get something more inspired to flow. I would also recommend that you set goals and find a way to make yourself accountable to them—the quantity of your writing will increase and you'll be happier for it!

Ernest Hemingway said, "Write drunk, edit sober." I'm not telling you to get hammered, but what he's really saying is that the first draft can be a mess. Everything works out in the editing… in fact, editing isn't complete until the story is polished. Another piece of advice I've often heard said is to "write for you—edit for your reader." Find what works for you—find your inspiration and method because at the end of the day, you are writing for you.

Playing with POV

I don't typically write in the first-person point of view, but some friends have tried it. They told me not to worry—they didn't inhale. I prefer to stick to the third person, but I've seen some very good stuff written through the eyes of the main character. That said, nearly everything that I've read outside of commercial, highly produced works have been done very, very poorly (and even a lot of traditional houses put out trash). Books suffering from POV problems have rarely suffered from the quality of the story. It's not always even about the writing quality—but rather a nuance of the POV.

Blogger/author Cayce Berryman writes a great article on the subject (http://www.cayceberryman.com/point-of-view-writing-in-first-person) and really puts a finger on it under the heading *Your Thoughts vs Their Thoughts*.

> "If you explain everything to your readers, you'll likely lose their interest, if not insult them. So, what's the solution? Let the main character be the eyes and ears, and let the reader be the brain... *I stared him down, hoping to make my point. "If you ever come near my kids again, I'll make sure you never see the light of day." His eyes widened and he backed away in fear.* I explained why I stared into his eyes as well as why he backed off. As the reader, you can figure out, for yourself, that I wanted to make a point when I said what I did."

It feels natural for us to insert those motivations to 1. make sure our point got across to the reader or 2. because we are used to explaining all sides of the narrative; the lines of this POV get blended when that happens.

I think this is what drags down the quality of those stories I mentioned above: we try to engage our readers in an intensely close POV, but then begin to silently narrate and push the reader out as we do.

That is helpful advice, and something writers often fail to consider. When we pull out of the established POV we actually turn off the readers by reminding them they are in a story rather than reality… it disrupts the flow and the magic of storytelling, even if only subconsciously.

Remember your readers and funnel everything through your character if you're using anything other than third person.

Genre Distinctions

Not everyone realizes that there is more to writing in a genre than just the content of a book or its tropes: fantasy stories have elves and dwarves and vampire fiction obviously has vampires in it. Romance should, likewise, focus primarily on the relationships within the story. That's all we need to know—time to pop out some books and get paid, right? Right? Not exactly.

Some of the finer genre nuances include voicing in your characters—the way they speak, the way they see the world, and what motivates them. This goes far beyond "typin die-log like dis if you was writtin a no good southern hornswaggler when'er yer heel is talkin." In fact, don't do that outside of a few rare exceptions. It makes reading terribly difficult for a reader if an entire character reads like that. It interrupts the flow—it is not at all what is meant by "voicing" a character.

Here's what I mean, when you are writing fantasy you may make up words or write mythopoeicly (world-building) which means you will pepper descriptions in or drop nuances through the story so that certain terms' meanings can be intuitively gleaned by context. For my Spec Fic YA novel, Wolf of the Tesseract I studied a few lists of things to keep in mind for my readers.

The primary YA audience is narcissistic by nature (it's not an insult, growing teens always go through a psychological stage where their thought process asks of everything, "what does this mean *to me?"*) For the novel, I intentionally funneled as much through the character's viewpoint as possible and lingered more on emotion than I normally would. I used more personal pronouns than I often might and was intentional about using accessible language (limiting "silver dollar" words without obvious context.)

Genre is about much more than just the thematic tropes. It is something that should be given forethought as you begin and when you edit a story. Always ask yourself how a reader will see your treatment of the text—for example, you may have written a romance novel meant for the female Christian market… if you write too explicitly or use profanity you can expect to turn off a huge segment of the readers (and expect bad reviews). Likewise, if you write a middle grade adventure but dwell too heavily on high prose as the child protagonist ponders psychological themes and motivations of the antagonists or the world which intersects his own, you will lose the reader. Things that work in the literary sphere don't work in an MG adventure novel, as a rule.

Literary fiction usually references "high concept" writing. It may have elements of genre stories. Think of the movie Gravity, for example (which was based on a script stolen from novelist Tess Gerritsen by legal loopholes). It involved astronauts and action in space, but the main point of the story was not the space-walk or an adventure—it was the theme of an invisible force calling us to overcome adversity and cling to life. That's a high-concept example making it literary rather than sci-fi.

Outside of "literary fiction" many individual thematic genres exist. Each one has its own set of rules (expected word count, appropriate styles and language, etc.) and should be researched. These include genre labels such as paranormal, horror, science fiction, fantasy, romance, western, nonfiction, commercial, crime, and so many more.)

Age genres will sometimes stack with thematic tags but help specify the *type* of target audience. YA novels are typically for teenagers while MG (middle grade) features stories written for 8-12 year olds. NA (new adult) targets readers around college age and is a fairly new segment recognized by the market; NA is primarily meant for 18-24 year olds.

Like all things, do your research so you can write the best book possible, and write to the rules rather than the exception for true success!

The Dangers of oversharing

I did an interview with <u>Pamela Jane</u>, an author of several children's books and a few memoir/lit ones. She is an author with books out through a few little companies like Random House, HarperCollins, and others. Pamela wrote an article about a personal experience with a major publisher.

Her article, titled <u>You Think it Can't Happen? How My Two Picture Books Were Stolen by a Major Publisher</u>, was published in Huffpo. It's worth a read, if nothing else as a cautionary tale. It might also demonstrate the protections that a literary agent provides to authors and serves as a reminder to document everything. The nuts and bolts of it is that she pitched an idea to the publishers who passed… big deal—happens all the time, but a while later the same publisher releases that exact book with a different writer—and it's accurate down to the details. It's a major fear we all have: someone else ripping off our content. It's an intellectual kidnapping.

Tess Gerritsen wrote a novel called Gravity which was optioned for a movie that she completed a screenplay for. The studio shutdown in a corporate acquisition and contracts were not transferred. The production team changed a few details on the script (namely, they erased her name) and they made a blockbuster for which she would not receive a dime (due to the legal chicanery of contract magic and business mergers.) Stuck in legal hell, she eventually gave up but warns authors on her website—be careful.

Writing is more than communication and entertainment. It's also a business and it's important to remember that individuals can be easily crushed beneath the wheels of industry. Don't be so afraid that you never take your ideas out for a test-drive… but don't be so foolish that you fail to wear your seat-belt, either.

Don't let paranoia control you and keep you from working with publishers… but also keep records and keep backups of everything! You never know when they might come in handy.

Faith-Based Predators

Thank God Tate is dead.

This article will probably be one of the first to become dated, but the principles will hold true. I happen to be a faith-based author, but the article applies to the secular as well.

Tate was one of the worst offenders of those businesses who preyed on Indies and strong-armed them into bad publishing deals—one of those vanity presses in disguise. They closed up shop shortly before Family Christian Stores shuttered every location of their brick and mortar super-chain in early 2017. Tate formally closed its doors on January 24, 2017. Good.

The unfortunate side of their story, however, is that Tate had long-broadcasted itself as a "Christian Company" as part of their lure to bring in authors whom they could take advantage of. Claiming to operate with a set of higher morals gets people to unwittingly drop their defenses.

The Christian market is a huge niche within the publishing sphere as a whole. With the closure of the industry's largest retail chain and other gaffes, it's bound to take a beating for years to come. Some of those gaffes might be what led to Tate's death: the major "Christian publishing houses" took Tate's modus operandi and began utilizing it, eating up their customer base. It's what Westbow Press, a division of Thomas Nelson and Zondervan (the biggest faith-based houses), has done—and mark my words, this will eventually come back up in publishing news.

While Tate is finally dead, there are still tons of clones out there ready to rip off indie authors, so use extreme prejudice when looking at "self-publishing services." Just because a company claims to operate off of a faith-based set of principles, that doesn't change the fact that they could be a predator. The difference between a lamb being eaten by atheist wolves and a lamb being eaten by "Christian" wolves is that the latter pack of animals says grace before devouring you. If you look up Westbow online you will find two things. 1. Accolades from the biggest and best in the Christian market, hoping association will rub off on the prodigal house. 2. Serious complaints and reports of abusive treatment and deceptive business practices.

Years ago, Tate tried *very* hard to sign me after writing my first novel. I was barely surviving on almost zero income and working as a broke youth pastor with two kids, a mortgage, a second job, and a church income of $50 per week. Tate was more than happy to pressure me into signing—but prayerful wisdom prevailed and I turned them down. I recognized that places like Tate stroke egos and dangle dreams and promises in front of writers. Luckily, I found horror stories on the Preditors and Editors website which helped steer me away from Tate and a few other companies who contacted me regarding my manuscript (as if publishers regularly email unknown writers or solicit submissions from them).

This industry is full of deceptive promises and broken dreams— even the Christian book market. As a writer, you have to be the primary driving energy behind your success—even huge traditional presses can't succeed if you don't bring that. Nobody has a greater interest in seeing your book succeed than *YOU*, so get out there and make it happen.

What about book size?

I've always been a story teller and remember a creative writing class in high school. Everyone groaned to learn that we had to write at least something one page long, printed, 12-point font, double-spaced. One classmate commented, "Of course Schmitz is gonna write at least ten pages and make us all look bad." Guilty as charged. But talking about size and length begs the question, *What defines a short story?*

I often refer to a list that I keep regarding definitions of stories by word lengths. We humans tend to judge things by comparison and so I'll add some famous story word lengths for you... but remember that word count is not a true measure of quality any more than weight is a measurement of beauty.

Completing a book sounds easier when you learn that the minimum word count of a Novel is probably less than you think. Comparison can be helpful. NaNoWriMo used to sound so impressive until I wrote half the requirements in less than 2 weeks after a bolt of inspiration.

Here are the story types based on word count
Novel: 40,000+
Novella: 17,500-40,000
Novelette: 7,500-17,500
Short Story: 1,000-7,500
Flash Fiction: 500-1,000 short stories often done as contests (including 6 word stories, twitter stories, etc.)

Many types of books' expected word counts vary depending on the specific genre. That said, it's important to note that it's virtually unheard of in our era to be traditionally published with a debut novel of over 150,000 words. PH.D. dissertations are typically limited to 100,000. My first novel was 175,000—I eventually rewrote it as two 100,000 word novels. Rein it in or break it up!

I think back to that high school experience nowadays and think, that requirement was only like 250 words. That's barely a Twitter rant by modern comparison. Here are some of your favorite modern and classic books by word length, starting with the largest English work for reference.

History of a Young Lady, Samuel Richardson, 985,000
Atlas Shrugged, Ayn Rand, 565,000
War and Peace, Leo Tolstoy, 560,000
Battlefield Earth, L. Ron Hubbard, 420,000
Harry Potter and the Sorcerer's Stone, J.K. Rowling, 77,000
Harry Potter and the Goblet of Fire, J.K. Rowling, 191,000
Hunger Games, Suzanne Collins, 100,000
The Maze Runner, James Dashner, 101,000
Twilight, Stephanie Meyers, 119,000
A Game of Thrones, George R.R. Martin, 293,000
The Fellowship of the Ring, J.R.R. Tolkien, 177,000
The Hobbit, J.R.R. Tolkien, 95,000
Nineteen Eighty-Four, George Orwell, 89,000
Ender's Game, Orson Scott Card, 101,000
The Lion the Witch and the Wardrobe, C.S. Lewis, 36,000
Old Yeller, Fred Gibson, 36,000
The Mouse and the Motorcycle, Beverly Cleary, 22,000

Hopefully this gives you some good reference points. Happy writing.

Do Your Homework

Before launching forward in your endeavor and actually paying any money to anyone for any service, you should count the cost. Know what your final cost is going to be on a product before you begin—it is important to know so you can determine your margin and cost. Even if for no other reason, it is an important part of setting your purchase price (which you should know early in order to put it on the back cover if you plan to meet industry standards.)

As an example of price comparison, I will give you a few cost analyses comparing the previously mentioned Westbow Press and then the same book printed through a truly Indie route.

For the sake of the argument, we will try to get packages as close to similar as possible. There will be a few differences. For instance, Westbow offers hardcovers but does not offer audiobook—outside of signing up for a "pay to publish" package I haven't found an economical way to get a hardcover without one by the time of this writing. If it is a deal breaker, the cheapest service I found has been Bookbaby where you can get a single hardcover printed for about $60-80 unless you paid for a package, then it's a little under half that depending on quantity ordered.

Our comparison book will be a hypothetical 160-page paperback in a 6x9 format and price it at 9.99. We will assume we need to hire an editor and purchase cover art in order to be fair, though it will be a more expensive publishing package in order to be more similar. Because reviews of Westbow's editing have proved horrendous, we will estimate a low price for editing services. For the sake of an argument, we will assume *no discounts* of any sort for either party.

Westbow "Online Platform"
Cost: $4,399

ISBN	included	Will get two in order to have hardcover edition
Alt. format: Hardcover	included	5x copies
Press Release	*	Package indicates a value, but no amount listed
Social media guide	*	Package indicates a value, but no amount listed
Promo materials	$720	300ea biz cards, postcards, bookmarks
Website	$599	No domain and limited TOS. Charges fee to update page.
Editing	$499	
Bookstub	included	10x (promo download card)
Cover Design	*	Package indicates a value, but no amount listed
Catalogue inclusion	included	Westbow Press (FYI I've never heard of this one)
Cost for 31x copies	*	Says "Free" (it's part of the cost of your package)
Westbow sets a higher price	$14.99	Retail Price
Profit per paperback	$1.49	Sold on Amazon
Cost per book	$10.49	Author copies at 30% off

you can check out package costs here:
http://www.westbowpress.com/Packages/PackageCompare.aspx

Indie method for same or better package
Cost: $622

ISBN	$10	Second ISBN needed for distributor returnability
Alt. format: Audiobook	$0	10x downloadable coupons on completion
Press Release	$5	Service via Fiverr
Social media guide	$0	Many guides online for free
Promo materials	$71	500 biz cards, 250 postcards, 1000 bookmarks
Website	$0	Comp to Wix free account— but you can update for free.
Editing	$200	Various places found online
Bookstub	$15	500x (made via Vistaprint with Smashwords coupons)
Cover Design	$150	A median price for high quality, Indie cover art
Catalogue inclusion	$85	Ingram Advance (a respected catalogue)
Cost for 31x copies	$86	Via Createspace
Indies retain control over product pricing	$9.99	Retail Price
Profit per paperback	3.22	Sold on Amazon
Cost per book	$2.77	Author copies at Createspace

Createspace creation calculator here:
https://www.createspace.com/Products/Book/

Analysis: you get a whole lot more for less cost to you *and* less cost to your buyers.

Pretty much everything they are claiming to do for that extra $4,000 from you (and the extra $5 from anyone who buys your book,) you can actually do for very little money *or* no money if you have some time and the drive to learn or refine a skill.

For a tenth of the cost you're getting almost triple the promo materials if you shop for yourself. Compare the percentage increase on bookstubs (which is not really a huge promo item in my experience.) Many of the services they pad the package price with are things that wind up on the list of purchases Indies regret even paying for. Press releases are irrelevant unless the author is already a bestseller or he or she is local—if you're local, write the thing yourself! You're a writer, aren't you? So, write something.

Catalogue inclusion? A phone call to bookstores within your hundred-mile radius will yield far better results, and might also earn you a book signing.

Price is also important. The last few lines show you the real rub and demands the research be done. Even with book prices a full third lower you make more than twice the royalties per book. Your cost per book is only 25% of the package deal… that means selling a person your Indie copy earns you over $7 and costs you less than three compared to a copy from Westbow which earns you $4.50 but costs you almost eleven bucks. Math doesn't lie.

There are a great many other factors that factor in to wisdom in going Indie… things like quality control, artistic control, price strategy, the fact that the "publisher wants to charge you to scan an image to upload to *your* website—and then charge you to update the website, and so much more. The flip side is true as well: some people would rather pay someone else to do it all for them. I can understand and respect that. But heck, I'll give you that exact package on the Indie side for half of what Westbow is charging! (I say that tongue in cheek—but I'd seriously put my skills to work if someone wanted to hire me for them. Look me up online to contact me—I'd even do a consultation for you if you needed some private guidance.)

I admit that I come out strongly against vanity presses—especially vanity presses that represent themselves as something more akin to an Indie publisher (there are *some* that call themselves co-publishers or hybrid publishers that can prove a happy medium—but you still need to do your homework and run the numbers.) I would take less issue with any company that charged (even as part of a publishing package) if they were truly geared towards making authors successful, but with the price margins set up the way they are, companies like Westbow are CERTAINLY trying to take advantage of enthusiastic Indies and use them as free marketing employees. This isn't just Westbow. It's everyone. It's why so much of this book talks about the issue. If I failed to warn about it… well, that'd be like the *actual* Bible not talking about sin.

Westbow is a "Christian Publisher," but Christian-book-publishing is just as secular as any other cut-throat business, regardless of the product's contents between the covers. I break down the publisher's details with a little more detail in my blog (basically, you have to sell almost a thousand books to be back at $0/break even and the company has profited over $15k.)

Until the co-publishing/price-sharing/self-publishing houses figure out that authors aren't stupid people they will continue running schemes and scams on us. Unfortunately, most starry-eyed first-timers are just happy to talk to a publisher (of any variety) and so they are easily suckered into agreements. Hopefully this gets you looking at doing your homework and shows you how to break down the details.

You should also watch out for other kinds of scams I've blogged about including purchasing email lists. Use a web search for every company by name to get reviews.

Remember, honest companies are willing to share more details. Dishonest companies use strong-arm tactics and manipulation (if they even respond at all!)

Adding Intentional diversity to your book

For all the talking about knowing your audience I do, it is worth keeping in mind that there can be times when harnessing aspects of different demographics can have powerful results and both help sell books as well as have a social impact. You might even deepen yourself as a writer and human as well.

Getting outside your own point of view is a great exercise in writing--and it goes beyond just race. Write outside your own gender or species even! As a matter of pure exercise, I wrote Piano of the Damned to do exactly that. While working as an Evangelical Christian youth pastor I put myself in the shoes of a gay pianist with mafia ties in the 1940s. That's a significant amount of degrees outside of my "native culture."

I don't put much stock in "white privilege" arguments (I think we're all equally messed up human beings and just in different ways) and I do my best to live life with race-blindness. (I'll refrain from talking specifics about my fairly diverse family and friendships as that has somehow become a part of white privilege, too.) Still, the advice in Upstart Crow's blog is good.

"The best story you can tell is your own story, one that speaks the truth about your experiences. One that translates your triumphs and failures into an unforgettable character."

Tell your story from your POV in the human condition, but don't be too scared to write characters from different points of view, too. Don't skimp on the research—if you have a black character or Asian one, find a friend with that background and get some feedback.

Coming at the diverse angle with an open mind and objective point of view is good. Demonstrate a desire to learn about different cultures and seek more than just a superficial treatment of it in your text, otherwise your characters will come off as caricatures. If you try to genuinely gain understanding from those points of view and build relationships in order to do that, you might just find your worldview changing, your interests broadened, and a whole new realm unveiled.

Remember, our humanity is the primary thing that binds us together. Use that well and everything will take on an air of authenticity—and maybe even make your story more accessible to readers with different cultural backgrounds.

The Black Moment

This is maybe my favorite thing about being a writer... "the black moment." I came across a nifty article recently about the subject over at <u>Rayne Hall's blog</u>.

The Black Moment is a descent into darkness – physical, emotional, mental, psychological, or spiritual, or even all of those. As a prime example, you could think of when Samwise Gamgee in Lord of the Rings believes that Frodo Baggins has been killed by the giant spider, Shelob. On the other end of the genre spectrum, (we'll look at Pride and Prejudice,) it might also be when Elizabeth believes all hope has passed for her and Mr. Darcy following her sister's scandalous elopement with Mr. Wickham. That ratcheted tension, and all the feels that accompany it, permeate the black moment.

Perhaps I have a streak of sadism, but I enjoy running my characters through grueling physical and emotional gauntlets. Bringing a character to the brink of breaking is a way to demonstrate ultimate strength or weakness. Stephen King and George R.R. Martin are also masters of this.

From the reader's point of view, it can feel like authors are heartless monsters who like toying with emotions. Sometimes we are. The black moment has to be intentional and not merely darkness for the sake of bloodshed. (There's a great comic online with a page looking like a children's book: the Grim Reaper is sitting on a park bench with bodies all around. He's saying, "oops," and the caption reads: *authors be like…*)

I've put a character through the wringer or even killed some—I've had angry calls and emails. Those moments of tension that nearly break the story can be critical to a memorable climax!

Here are some great elements that can help increase that tension in a story's plot:

1. Betrayal by a friend
2. Becoming hopelessly lost or stranded
3. A loved one in danger
4. Someone important dies (a mentor, friend, family, etc.)
5. A time limit raises the stakes
6. A love interest goes cold (even divorce)
7. One more unmentioned task is given to the characters and it is impossible
8. Something secret and hidden about a protagonist is revealed
9. An early encounter with the villain demonstrates he/she is unbeatable
10. A devastating choice is laid upon the hero who will feel responsible for the fallout of one option over another

Don't skimp on the turmoil and check out Rayne's blog for some other great advice on situations and nuances to increase the intensity of the effect. Without tension and escalating black moments there is no such thing as a "page turner."

Passivity/Copulation

Noooo... not that kind of copulation! I'm not much for the ripped bodice genre.

I read a great article about the Copula: "the connecting link between subject and predicate of a proposition." I'll clarify that in a second. The copula is the bane of all new writers out there and it is especially notorious among Indie/self-published authors. A copula is usually found as a use of any form of "to be" in your writing; this would include: was, is, will be, was, were, had been, became, was, was being, and was. In fiction, I hate "was" so badly that it hurts.

If there is any single piece of writing advice I could ever give it is this: reduce passive verbs to no more than one per three pages. It's a trap—using *was* is sloppy and undisciplined writing. It can be especially deadly if you are trying to increase tension. It's an easy trap to fall into—tighten those sentences up and look for copulas in your revisions.

Using passive verbs really is the worst thing inexperienced writers do (I was a chief offender when I began to cut my own teeth with my first couple books.) The good news is that newer drafts can correct tedious and bland action verbs and the more you revise to fix older writing the more you will improve until you eventually avoid the copula as a habit—automatically opting for stronger verbs in the earlier manuscripts.

I spent years trying to reduce my own tendencies towards passive writing for fiction (nonfiction, especially journalism, has quite different rules for writing.) I edited a piece for a user on Absolutewrite's forum last year with a LBL (line by line critique) and had no choice but tell them they needed to scrap the whole thing, encouraging them to instead write five new works between 500-2500 words with the intent of honing their skill at editing, style, and removing "was" and passive verbs. The forums erupted with hate for me as if I was some kind of grammatical Prince Joffrey (never let your close friends be your final editors unless you want to be lied to). I highlighted the passive verbs in the first four sentences and did the math: I counted 27 verbs (one sentence ran overly long) and 21 of the verbs were passive!

The first response by another critiquer after explaining why we avoid passive verbs (bogs the sentence down, disinterests reader, lazy writing, etc.) was, "That's not what passive voice means!" I copied/pasted/posted the definition and muttered *"millennials"* under my breath. Needless to say, I don't bother editing on AW anymore. It's a great site, but too many chefs tweaking the broth for me.

> I often demonstrate a poorly written, passive sentence and a concise correction as an example.
>
> "John was running in a race and his opponent was running fast—but john was faster."
>
> "John   ran   fastest   and   won   the   race." The old adage is, *show, don't tell.* Showing draws us in making us active participants rather than someone being put to sleep by a second-hand account.

If Indie authors are going to get mainstream respect, we've got to drum out poor writing--that means begging with, pleading with, or murdering the worst offenders who drag down the quality quotient of the publishing world. It's important.

Here's a great article about the copula:
http://woodwardpress.com/2016/04/04/the-case-of-the-copula-overdose/

The Best Way to Get Better

Congratulations. You wrote a book. Now the actual work begins... and not just the editing—but everything else, too. For writers, the storytelling is the easiest part (at least it's the most driven part.)

The next thing I'm about to say will be difficult to hear for some people: if this is your first book, the overwhelming odds are that it's not very good. I say that from looking at numbers and statistics as well as my own experiences (including *my* first novel!) Nobody becomes an Olympic lifter after a week in the weight room (even if you're the strongest person at your gym—you're still not ready yet.) Writing is a craft and a skill that develops with time and practice. But there's some good news: it's relatively easy to get better... the best way to become a better writer is to write. And then write some more.

If you want to make the step from "writer" to "good writer," I'd recommend following what I did. I say that not from vanity, but because I know it works.

After completing my fantasy epic that nobody read called "The Kakos Realm, Book 1," I joined a writer's circle. I quickly learned that I'd done everything wrong—even though I'd somehow managed to sell my book to a small traditional press (which is no longer in business—that part might be relevant.) I learned that my book was 50,000 words longer than books were allowed to be. I also learned that my writing was not all that great (even if my storytelling was decent—there's a difference.)

In that time, I also discovered a fairly active online community for short fiction, critiques, magazine submissions, etc. and I began writing shorter pieces. And the criticism kept pouring in. I wrote more, and still stumbled over some of the same issues in my writing (the same issues that plague newer writers such as passive verbs, as-you-know-bob/info-dumps, and excessive descriptions.) My writers group cared enough to tell me and point out my flaws. Luckily, I also learned where I was good: plot twists, devices, and dialogue.

But criticism hurts. A lot. Criticism sucks, but it helped refine my art and craft to something that I'm happy with. It reveals strengths *and* weaknesses.

After more than three years of writing nothing other than short fiction I felt like I'd arrived at a better place. I learned a few important things in that era (and published like 30 short stories and wrote many others, even co-editing an anthology.) I learned how to start a story and set a hook. Writing with hard word-count limits taught me to write succinctly and how to cut extraneous material. I learned how develop characters and how to end a story. I learned how to tighten sentences so that they read with a cadence and flow. I learned how to edit, redraft, summarize, and submit stories. The editing alone is huge!

If you want to be a better writer, first go small. Focus in on a few short-fiction projects, even if just for the sake of improving your craft (write a few pieces for contests—find a secondary purpose if you need one—but you really ought to write some short things in order to improve your writing, hone your craft, and exercise your skills.)

Here are the next follow-up steps to add after you feel as if you've become proficient in learning to start a story, handle the plot elements, eliminate passive verbs, hook readers, write tight dialogue, and end the tale.

1. Go to writer's conferences. There are many other things other than writing a story (but also story elements) that you can pick up at a convention or conference… even if it's just to network you should try going to one a year. Invest in yourself. Your writing will be better for it.

2. Get involved in a writer's circle. You need objective feedback and peers who both know your struggle and can help you with crucial aspects of writing like beta reading, etc.
3. Give people permission to be honest about your stories and ask for feedback.
4. Encourage other authors and professionals while thinking towards your platform, mailing lists, etc. (even if you are years away from publishing.)
5. Decide if the Indie avenue is the best fit for you—maybe you are already dead set on the traditional path… examine the possibilities and what it means if that door never opens.

Being an author isn't really that easy. It's a burden like a fire trapped in your bones. Especially fiction authors, you carry the tales and lives of thousands of fictional people shut up in your soul—if you do not tell their story, they will never get to exist. Put in the effort to do it right; your characters demand it. Strive for excellence.

Write well! Made up lives hang in the balance.

Why People Think Indies are Turds in the Swimming Pool

I read lots of Indie and self-published books to review on my blog (usually at least 40 per year). I want to be serious about why most people are gun-shy about reading Indie and self-pubbed books. Quite honestly, it's not because readers like what the major houses sell (quite honestly, they push a limited spectrum of voices that *do not* always represent peoples' desires and interests.) It is because too many writers are not authors—rather, they are people who wanted to see their name on a book.

Too many people refuse to edit, redraft, or fail to put serious effort into their work. Some have been lured in by promises of vanity-press companies that seem to promise their book will be the next best-seller and then call them "Indies." Shoddy books are easy to identify: unrefined cover art done by Deviant-art users with portfolios filled with anthro/furry erotica; stock art or poor 3d CGI background shots that are unrelated to the book; Title/Text featuring the Papyrus font; nonstandard book details; high retail price; and more (I write about it elsewhere in detail.)

Those "publishing houses" are typically geared to make money off of authors and not sales, so they don't care—their soul isn't invested in the book, so they are not true Indies, they already broke even by selling author services. For those publishers, the status quo is "good enough that the author sends a check" resulting in another crappy Amazon book going live... don't be that guy or girl. Don't publish until your book is a highly crafted piece that's ready for the market. For real Indies, the investment level is *high* and the status quo is never quite within your grasp.

I've picked up many of these crappy books at small bookshops, turned the spine to find Xulon, Tate Publishing, Createspace, etc. and felt compelled to find a restroom in order to wash my hands off. Some companies and some authors are *downright terrible*. BUT NOT ALL OF THEM ARE—unfortunately, we're all in this together. It only takes a couple kids pooping in the swimming pool to make the rest of the waters nasty for the rest of us.

Some authors do things right and I have contacted some writers directly because the marketing was so good that, at first glance I could not honestly tell whether or not it was put out by an Indie or by a major publishing house. That leads me here: <u>an article by Lindsay Buroker about Amazon's marketing/advertising.</u>

I like Lindsay Buroker she breaks down some analysis for a break-even point on some of her sales using a structure that pays per clicks and shows her profitability. Quality books and quality marketing will make readers second guess any bias against Indie titles. When an author is serious enough to actually invest in marketing strategies, they are likely to make sure it's right—and if not, they will put in the energy to fix it.

Indies ought to be intolerant. Always be improving, setting the bar higher, and stand firm against poop smears on the diving board.

Stay out of the end of the pool with all the brown floaters.

Four Things to Watch For When Self-Editing

Because I do book reviews I often check in on what other people think of books that I see eye-catching ads for or if they have extremely brutal or stellar reviews. I know this seems like an odd way to start an article about self-editing, right? Just bear with me.

One particular fantasy book series that was creeping up on ten books had amassed a *lot* of reviews and criticism. I actually started looking under the hood (so to speak) of the author's operation for two reasons: 1) the top Facebook response was an attack because the advertisement had stolen a screen-grab of Gallifrey as its image (Dr. Who's home planet, for the non-SF crowd,) and that got my interest up. 2) despite so many legitimate complaints, there were still many sales (though a huge number were freebie/giveaway.) The high number of reviews interested me. This writer was a regular guy, just like me, banging the keys at his kitchen table. How could such a lackluster author amass such a following?

Many of the complaints circled some very real issues and legitimate complaints: The author changed the spelling of a minor character's name at some point mid-series. The timeline was out of whack in some others where the author obviously cut and pasted a large section and messed with the continuity without editing for content. One character who had previously died was suddenly alive again for a scene. And the grammar… doing grammar un goodly will makes mad peoples'—a large number of reviewers suggested that the writer never did more than a first draft before going straight to self-publishing with and writing the next installment. Poor technical writing defeats any immersive, world-building stories.

Editing is not optional and, unless you're made of money and have an editing team willing to spend weeks rewriting someone else's content, everyone needs to self-edit.

Self-editing is something that all writers ought to do after the first draft is complete. Also, I shouldn't have to say it, but *it is not sufficient to rely on for your final draft.* Get fresh eyes at some point down the line. Here are a couple key problems writers make in rough drafts and some easy tools to help overcome them.

Continuity errors: screwing up the timeline/order of events. Draw a timeline to help track *when* things happen. Also, write an outline—even if you don't use one to write, use it to edit—go back and write an outline after the fact to help spot errors.

Character issues (descriptions, personality traits, purpose to the plot arc): keep a dossier or dramatis personae as if you were writing a wiki for your world. Mark when the character is killed, affiliations, etc. so that you don't change a minor character midstream. Again, you can do this after the first draft and use it to edit.

Grammar errors: there are two ways to tighten this up 1) don't make errors and always write well the first time… but since you're not a robot, 2) have people who will help spot errors and fix them. Aim for #1, but know that your writing will never be perfect, so rely heavily on #2. Skill is earned by editing and learning from mistakes… they don't have to be your own errors, either. You can refine skills by peer editing the works of other authors—find a writing group to connect with!

Telepoofing: this is that writing magic that comes from suspending disbelief and we see it all the time in Hollywood. The bad guy has the cure to the disease that will kill our hero in 24 hours and the villain, after infecting your west-coast main character, Bob Robertson, evil Dr. McMeanypants fled to his secret lair in Europe back in chapter five. After the rest of the events (discovering the location, a brief romantic interlude, a stopover at the CDC, and a cute scene where the protagonist rescues a batch of kittens), the story climaxes—Bob has to get the cure or die when "Poof!" he's teleported to Europe in search of Dr. McMeanypants's hideout in between chapters. The action takes place "off camera" and the story goes on... but even a nonstop flight from L.A to Europe will take *at least* 16 hours. Sometimes you can get away with things, but understand that you can only push the envelope of your details so much. Writing a timeline and outline will help here, too, depending on what details you pay attention to. If there is a timer on a plot point (poison, bomb, etc.) pay attention to the clock. If there is a supernatural thing at play (vampires, werewolves, etc.) pay attention to when the sun goes down and the moon or astronomical phases. If you mention guns being fired, get your calibers and ammo types right (shotguns won't kill people beyond close range and a .22 is not a sniper rifle). Remember that *the devil is in the details.*

Self-editing tip: If you mention specific details or if certain details are essential to the plot make sure they are right. Do some research—even for fiction! Nonspecific information can be covered below a thin veneer of vagueness and left to the reader's assumption... a limp is a great character detail but you don't need to mention which leg it is, or reference it frequently... not every character in your world needs or deserves a detailed description of their complexion, hair color, dental alignment, etc. Readers will fill in the details, let them partner with your story and immerse themselves in it. They will make assumptions about what a house looks like, or what kind of car someone drives, etc. Don't describe what they are seeing from an outside perspective, tighten your writing skill and loosen your descriptors so that readers experience your world from within the fourth wall, rather than from the outside.

The Most Useful Tips for Self-Editing Manuscripts

First, let me say this. Always always always get an editor.

Do not make the mistake of taking a *highly self-edited* manuscript to publishing if you have the option a *marginally self-edited* work with a mediocre *paid edit* for your manuscript. The second option will nearly always yield a better result. ALWAYS factor in a budget (even if only a small one) into your publishing scheme— always plan to pay for editing (even if it's just $100 to a 4th year English Major).

The thing you are looking for most is an objective perspective. One thing editors at various conferences and conventions talk about is "distance from the story." Nobody knows your story like you do—I've often discovered that what editors say is true about reading your story: you read what you meant to write, especially if you wrote it recently. Editors and veteran writers talk about "putting a manuscript in a drawer" or letting the completed story "simmer" until it's ready. If you've edited, critiqued, or beta read for fellow authors you may understand what I'm talking about... it's easier to spot flaws when the text is new to you or when you are unfamiliar with it. Cold detachment is the best way to have that objectivity, so here are five techniques to simulate that and make your self-edits better.

1. Take some time to get distance from the manuscript. The longer the better, in essence--although you still want to be familiar with your story (five months may be fine; five years may be too long). You don't want your mind filling in blanks between omitted words with text that might not actually exist. You also want some of the plot points to be relatively new to your mind (surprise yourself with the plot

twists you previously wrote, if possible.) You are too close to the story to begin editing immediately after completion. Let it stew on the back-burner for a bit.

2. Use a different font. Anything to make it less familiar will help your brain spot errors and inconsistencies. I'd recommend Courier New or another monospaced font. When every letter of the word shifts to the same width it can change the structure of the text and make your mind have to process the "sight words" rather than just fill-in-the-blanks.

3. Read the text aloud. I use this one a lot. It really does help me spot errors, especially in line editing. Although it's not a perfect method, it never fails to help me discover omitted words or clunky language.

4. Work from a printed copy. Sometimes holding it, seeing it, and feeling the text can add a new dimension. It can also help by giving you scratch paper to jot notes in the margins, highlight, etc. Personally, I prefer to do this and often load a work in progress into my Createspace account and print WIP versions of my novel for my beta readers. I encourage them to write on the pages, highlight, and cross out words so that I can make a stronger version at my next pass.

5. Read the paragraphs backwards to forwards. Hop to the end of a chapter and work backwards paragraph by paragraph. This helps isolate the text and disrupts the story continuity enough to help you locate errors and make corrections, but not so much that the editing can't be done.

I hope these tips help; happy editing!

What if my story's title is already used?

"What if my book title is the same as one that's already in print?" It's not uncommon to wonder—especially in light of how many books are published every year. We can't keep getting longer and longer titles—we'd run out of cover space.

As a quick sample, hop on Goodreads and search for the title "Cursed." As I write this, 83 pages of results come up with a title that includes the word "Cursed." On just the first page there are 9 books whose full title is *Cursed.*

Sharing a title could come down to a trademark issue if you were obviously trying to infringe on someone else's intellectual property for personal gain. I don't know the actual laws and I'm neither a lawyer nor a vampire, so don't rely on me for legal advice. However, having the same title as another book is not as big of a deal as someone might think... that said, I wouldn't recommend you go out and write a blatant rip off story about a little boy named Larry Podder who has a star-shaped scar over his eye and discovers that he's a wizard. There're enough of those already and J.K Rowling has a dungeon full of captured plagiarists her minions have absconded with. A lot of it comes down to obvious intent.

Here's a good piece of advice lifted from Cayce Berryman's blog (http://cayceberryman.com)
"According to Circular 34, works as short as book titles cannot be copyrighted, which technically means you are able to use it. This can be confusing for your audience, however, as well as the audience of another author. This might seem exciting if you have a book with a similar title as a more successful author, but do you really want to subject yourself to hiding under their umbrella? For

that matter, do you want to risk the loophole that could get you in a lot of trouble?"

I agree with that last line. Be original and stand out. It will prove better in the long haul, but especially when you have a short, powerful word as a title don't fret over other books sharing a name. Look at the music industry, Wikipedia shows five albums titled Broken have been released since I was a teenager and 26 songs have been named the same.

I would recommend reading into if it's a major concern of yours. If you look through my blog you'll probably see the posts from when someone tried to steal one of my stories and release it as their own. Don't even mess with infringement, but if you are trying to be careful and have a genuine concern, then you're probably not infringing on anybody, as demonstrable by the fact that you care.

Again, if it's a serious concern do your due diligence. I would certainly encourage you to consult a lawyer for specific legal questions.

Size Matters

You are a writer. You put words on paper to satisfy that inexorable need burning within your soul. Guess what: nobody cares.

I know, that sounds crass and even rude—but there are some hard truths to learn about the publishing industry. Mostly gone are the days of high-falutin literary fiction novels meant to examine the human condition in painfully drawn-out purple prose. I have mixed feelings about that, but one thing is true: this is a business and businesses are concerned with what they can make a profit off of. You might have the best novel ever, written with words that pierce the heart and sunder the soul. If it won't sell, there's no point and purpose as far as the industry is concerned and you may have been better off becoming a preacher than a writer.

Because of the nature of business wanting to maximize its profits, you might have a book that sells reasonably well, but it still gets no respect from the shelves of bookstores, or even from publishers and agents. It is more economical for publishers, book buyers/distributers, and bookstores to produce, assemble, and store for resale shorter books rather than longer ones. Think about it: it costs more to pay for editors for a 400-page book compared with a 200-page one—the same goes for ink, glue, and paper used to create it.

Business economics rules the bookstore. If you have a 6x9 $19.99 600-page book for sale and it sits on a shelf stacked two deep and sells both copies in a day, that's $40. If that same title is competing for an equally popular 6x9 $12.99 200-page book, that shelf space can now gross $78 and not require constant restocking. These are the little details that writers don't usually think about tend not to understand. Bookstores don't care if your writing is superior or if you're the next big thing: what matters most is the price per square inch your titles can make them at the end of the fiscal quarter. It's callous and cruel—but there is very little room for art in business… if you understand this model as you format and write, you can mitigate the potential emotional fall-out from the cruel nature of the world.

I made the mistake of writing a 200,000-word epic right out of the gates. It's a real rookie mistake but one common to people who write with passion: stories burn within them and they have more desire to write than to do research on market norms or try to understand the publishing world. However, it shows a level of professionalism when writers know and understand the generally recognized market guidelines.

Because consumers have generally accepted market norms based on different genres, the *type* of book you write will dictate what is considered an acceptable word length. Nobody wants a 40,000-word fantasy epic. That's too short, but might be perfect for a corset-ripping romance or a YA book.

Typically, the maximum word count of ANY book caps out at 150,000. Rules can be broken (especially if your name is King, Martin, Rowling, etc. and you have a proven track record of topping the bestsellers chart. My advice is to be the rule, rather than the exception. Playing by the rules will save you much frustration in the long run). Following is a list of a generally acceptable minimum/maximum word count to use as a guide (plus or minus 5,000-10,000 words is generally fine.)

Literary, Commercial, Women's fiction: 80,000 to 110,000 – larger size is typically better.

Crime Fiction: 90,000 to 100,000

Mysteries, Thrillers, Suspense: 70,000 to 90,000 – Cozy Mysteries are on the shorter end of the spectrum and more serious ones should steer towards the deeper end.

Romance: 40,000 to 100,000 – "The sweet spot is in the middle" …which is also the title I will use if I ever decide to write a bodice-ripping romance story.

Fantasy: 90,000 to 140,000 – about 100,000 is a good place to start. Readers expect a thick read and anything less than 90,000 might not get a second look.

Paranormal: 75,000 to 95,000

Horror: 80,000 to 100,000

Science-Fiction: 90,000 to 125,000

Historical: 100,000 to 120,000

Young Adult Fiction (YA): 50,000 to 80,000

New Adult Fiction: 60,000 to 85,000

Middle Grade: 25,000 to 40,000

Picture Books: 500 to 700

Because of the fact that this is a business, I would be careful to balance my formatting against whitespace and the layout/line spacing of my printed book. If you can shrink the spacing down without causing eyestrain for a reader or without running sentences right up to the edge of the paper, it's worth looking into. From a purely economic perspective, shrinking line spacing from 1.5 to 1.15 can prevent waste and still produce an impressive book. Experiment, but be smart.

Indicators of Fake Writing Contests

Social media is a powerful tool. It can be a boon to those with something to advertise and can prove beneficial to savvy Indies who use that route to market their books. It can also be a way for predators to hoodwink authors into really bad deals. While there is no end to the "writing classes," "publishers," and "author services" that will pop up in your feeds because of targeted marketing, you will also see a number of "writing contests" promising you the world as long as you submit right away (like, before you have time to research the contest and learn that it's bogus.)

Many of the contests that I see listed as "sponsored posts" on Facebook (advertisements) are total shams. Take it from me, a guy who's been suckered by a couple of them when I went through my "let's enter a bunch of contests" phase, many of them have some pretty bad crap in the Terms of Service/small print. For example, one such contest reserved the electronic print rights of ALL submissions for several YEARS. Before you enter *any* contest, make sure you look under the hood and do your homework on the program itself.

Here are some signs that the contest you are thinking about entering bears further investigation:

•Its name is very close to a more well-known contest

•You have to purchase additional author packages (or it is strongly suggested) for services of any kind or must purchase copies of your own work (like anthologies)

•Contest's page is listed in Google as a possible scam, or has negative marks in Predators and Editors/Writer's Beware (http://pred-ed.com/) or Winning Writers (https://winningwriters.com/the-best-free-literary-contests/contests-to-avoid)

•Low standards (everyone gets in) and/or the contest is popularity based (measured by the amount of clicks/traffic a story produces)

•Contest is free but writers must pay high prices to purchase personal copies

•Unusually high promised prize money

•Contest hosts are unusually slow to respond to questions or don't respond at all

•It is hard to find info on past winners

•Contest judges have suspicious, illegitimate, or *no* qualifications

•Winners or "qualified entrants" are promised entry into an anthology (and the word limit is usually very low)

•The "prize" is something that will actually cost money or is intangible (like agency representation from a company with no real credibility)

•Top prizes are only awarded if you pay to attend a conference or convention to receive it

•Published bio or extra info in an anthology alongside your work costs additional monies

•You feel a contest representative is trying to coerce you for any reason or make promises

•They try and sell you a "publishing package" or state that such a package is worth $XYZ in prize money

•You give up any kind rights for submitting (but not necessarily for publishing, which may be a later step)

•You have to subscribe to anything to enter or "subscription is included in the entry cost"

•The contest is sponsored by a publisher that turns up scam warnings with a quick web search

•The publisher heaps uninvited praise on your submission

•The contest was advertised in a venue unrelated to publishing (Facebook, newspaper, popup ad, etc.)

These signs don't necessarily mean that a contest is a scam—but it certainly puts up a red flag and tells you to do some research. There are lots of phonies out there, look for signs and enter contests with a healthy dose of realism and skepticism.

Pros and Cons of Indie vs. Traditional Publishing

Traditional Publishing is recognized as that world where a writer submits his book to a trade publishing house and gets a "book deal." The book is revised, contracts signed, and then the publisher is responsible for all of the production costs, distribution, and sales. Based on their pay structure, they cut the author a royalty check based on the contract's terms. Up until Indie publishing became a real thing, this was always known simply as "Publishing." Because there was no secondary model, there was no need for a distinction.

Indie Publishing is a relatively new world where artists can color outside of the lines to varying degrees. It usually refers to self-published writers who effectively act as their own publisher, doing all of the things a trade house normally does but with stylistic freedom enough to try new things. This term may also include many smaller "Indie Publishing Houses" that, as a small business, act as a publisher that might be unrecognized by the larger industry. We rarely use the word "self-publish" because of how stigmatized the word has become (usually reserving it for Vanity Press publishers.) Indies reserve complete creative and financial control of their books and are often more artisanal than commercial.

Vanity Publishing is the kind of press that exists to create books that someone wants to see in print in order to make themselves feel good (vanity/self-validation), give as a gift, or for something like a school or church fundraiser, etc. These places serve an actual purpose (making church cookbooks or printing school yearbooks, etc.) but some have disguised themselves as traditional publishers, indie publishers, or "hybrid publishers" in order to prey upon Indie authors. *Vanity Publishers make their money off of the author rather than off of the book* (but still hope to skim a percentage off the top as well.) Avoid any "publisher" who wants to sell you a "publishing package" or makes their money off of author services. We won't dignify shady publishers them with our below comparison; they should be avoided and I write elsewhere about them in detail.

The difference between Indie and Traditional might be something like being on a company payroll versus being a private contractor. When you have a boss, manager, or foreman you have to do things *his or her way.* They may or may not like your own creative approach to the job and can tell you to change it. A private contractor can say, "This is how I'm doing it—if you don't like it, don't hire me for your next job;" they only get to eat when they work, so they have to stay hungry in order to make the house payment.

There are some strengths and weaknesses to each. You ought to go into publishing your materials with a clear idea of what you are getting into so you can choose which model best fits you. Here are a few lists to contrast and compare:

Pros:

Traditional	Indie
Prestige and Validation	Creative control
Store distribution is easy	High royalty rates
Work with a professional team	Quick Payments
No upfront fees/costs	Faster time to market
Possible advance on royalties	Control over format, rights, etc.
Literary prize potential	
Easier to become a "name brand" author	

Cons:

Traditional	Indie
Very slow process	Do everything yourself
Loss of creative control	No prestige
Low royalty rates	Difficulty getting on store
Lack of *significant* marketing	shelves
help	Assume all financial risk
Possible contract issues	Lack of *any* marketing

(marketing is sticky for either side in today's paradigm)

Every author has to decide what he or she really wants out of being an author. For many, the Indie route will be a stepping stone that helps build a platform for success. For others, it is the only way they would ever want to go. Some are "traditional only." All of those are personal choices and either is perfectly fine. Many well-known authors have chosen to do both. They will have some self-published books along with some traditional titles to maximize how much they make from their labors. Think about it, people don't buy books based on the publishing house—they buy based on the author—his or her name is the brand. Some of these authors will even sign contracts for a book's US rights and then use the Indie route for worldwide or overseas sales to maximize all marketing opportunities and capitalize on consumer interest. Indies have to stay smart.

At the end of the day, choosing a side boils down to two things: creative control and money. At least at some level, money is always important… you can negotiate creative aspects or walk away deals based on your heart, but money is set in stone. Printers and distributors *must* get paid… unless you're cool with writing your next manuscript from the big-house.

I know a few Indies who sell about a hundred books a month with their online sales. They've created a demand and their audience is responding. That is a pretty high number, to be honest, but it is perfectly achievable with a lot of sweat and tears. Indies make about $4 per book (an average I've found to be about right) across the 3 major mediums. That's $4,800 per year and 1,200 books sold. A big name in writing might make over a dollar per book with a traditional press, but the more unknown authors make more like 75 cents per book sold. Those same sales numbers net the writer less than a grand given a traditional route.

Authors must always stay on top of things, regardless of the publishing model. One of my traditional publishers made some contract changes saying it would be more profitable if I signed an addendum. I should have had an agent take a look—my royalties on my last check were reduced to about a quarter per book. The above numbers would earn me just three hundred bucks. For a year's worth of sales and over a thousand sold (that's a 1,600% decrease in profitability, for the math nerds.)

Do your homework and be informed to avoid learning lessons the hard way. Everyone needs to make those decisions sooner and rather than later, but ultimately, there is no right or wrong answer. It's more of a spectrum—choose which model is best for you, just do so wisely.

Rejection

Sharing yourself—whether it's your stories as an author, your graphics or music as an artist, or yourself as a human in a relationship means you will all incur rejection of some sort or another. Not *everyone* will like you or your products. Truth be told—your book was probably not ready when you thought it was… think about it in the dating context: were you a good fit to marry when you first began dating? Probably not.

Most writers pursuing a traditional route begin querying agents and publishers long before they are ready. Sometimes rejection comes because we query a market that has been exhausted with similar stories or a story is simply not interesting to the buying market at that time. (I'm going to just leave this comment here and then assume this is not you… *most people who experience rejection and then go to self-publish do so because their writing wasn't refined enough…* They didn't hire editors, pour blood and sweat into multiple drafts—the end result wasn't up to snuff.)

Taking your ideas out into the literary world is not for the faint of heart. MAKE SURE THAT YOUR STORY IS READY BEFORE YOU PITCH IT! Also, especially if you're a nonfiction writer, make sure there is an audience for it!

I used to work in a pretty tough sales job—the company specialized in pitch work and had extremely high demands and quotas (I've heard they are toughest company to get hired on at as far as their field sales reps go.) Their intense sales training (which included some great psychological studies on salesmanship) was extremely beneficial. Something they drilled into their teams was that rejection happens all the time. More often than not, in fact. Reset immediately. Forget about it. You could've been on the verge of a sale and made a customer emotionally invested when they suddenly pull the pin or bail on a promise they made to buy. There's another customer around the bend. Immediately put yourself out there again—the product is great, everyone needs one, and you do them a disservice if you don't try to make them buy it. Shake it off.

Most of their sales force worked in high-stress, loud environments and most people weren't there to see *you*. The trick to selling, besides having a good product and the ability to physically perform, is having the grit to take rejection over and over and over. Literally, hundreds of rejections per day—thousands over the course of each job. If your self-worth is tied up in someone else embracing you and your product (your book in this case) then you're going to have a tough time.

My rejection pile is big. I've had both form rejections and excited agents or publishers who just weren't quite ready to sign me. You've got to compartmentalize those emotions. Understand that this is a business and that you make a product—make your query process somewhat mechanical and do it because it's on your schedule. Do it even when your heart's not in it (just write the query when it was).

Don't stop with this advice. Take a class on querying and even pay for professional feedback and guidance.

Grow thick skin. You have personal preferences. Expect that agents and publishers will as well. Believe in yourself and surround yourself with people who can be your cheerleaders... but if all of your beta readers think something needs work (or if you haven't told them to switch lasers from stun to kill) then you should still be at the drawing board, not submitting manuscripts to agents. Put your best foot forward, after all.

Rejection be damned—you're a writer. You got this. Keep writing. Keep editing. Keep querying.

Twitter Pitching

If you're like me and spend a lot more time *making* new worlds than engaging in the real one, you might have to be intentional about staying up to speed on things.

Last year I went to a writer's conference in Boston hosted by @ChuckSambuchino who produces the annual Writer's Market guide to publishers and literary agents. When he asked who was familiar with things like #pitpub, #pitmad, or #pit2pub I suddenly realized how bad I am at utilizing Twitter.

While getting ready to attend a MN Writers Workshop in St Paul I realized I'd better start utilizing Twitter. I still don't know as much about Twitter or about #pitchwars kinds of submissions events but I consider myself a real author and so I thought I'd look into it more.

Basically, you include the hashtag with a single tweet during which you pitch the book. During the events, publishers and literary agent's lookup the hashtag info and read your tweets. If they are interested they will contact you. It's easy in concept—but distilling a novel into hook with less than 160 characters is harder than it looks. But still, give it a try!

If you are in the dark like I was, you might check out these links to know more.
Here are 3 great resources on the topic:
https://novelpitch.com/tag/pitmad/ info and advice
http://carissa-taylor.blogspot.com/2013/01/contest-madness.html
pitch contest schedule
http://carissa-taylor.blogspot.com/2013/01/contest-madness.html
pitch wars info/home

Advice from a literary agent

Asking questions helps to get the pulse of literary agents. It doesn't guarantee any success, of course, but it certainly helps learn more about agents' expectations. Jennie Goloboy of Red Sofa Literary responded with 3 things to keep in mind when pitching an agent.

#1 Know that it's not about you. Agents/editors only will take on work that reflects a need on their list. This one is new to me and, while I knew it deep down, I'd never looked at it that way. I'd always heard that "agents take projects they feel passionate about and believe they can sell," but I never looked at it from the hardest end of the business spectrum—they snap up something most quickly if they've got it all-but-sold based on their individual connections.

#2 A big don't: don't memorize your pitch and then say it as fast as humanly possible. She's not saying *not* to memorize it; she's saying not to be wound so tightly that you blow through your pitch in twenty seconds and then sit awkwardly for the next nine minutes. Relax and remember that your job as an author is to be an expert communicator, so chill out and communicate effectively. Have trouble relaxing? I've heard social lubricants, if that's your thing, can take the edge off ;) just don't over-do it. The point is to find a way to be chill. Don't plan the pitch word for word, but know it deep down in your soul and then communicate your heart.

#3 If they don't take your project, ask if they have any advice for you. Use that time! I've done this. Remember that you paid for a block of time to pitch (at least that is the norm at most writers' conferences). Use that time wisely. You've essentially hired an

agent for a 10-15 minute block for feedback. It's not a lot of time and agents will have limited exposure to your manuscript/story, but they can give insight to your hook, layout, tightness of writing, and whether or not there is a current demand for the kind of story you have written.

Congratulations, a Publisher Signed You—Wait for The Other Shoe to Drop

That moment that a publisher says yes is an emotional moment. You're probably riding on cloud nine… even if it's not a well-known publisher. It is a deeply validating thing to be told "yes, we want you." Many less than scrupulous "publishers" take advantage of that sentiment and offer really bad contracts. This is the very reason that literary agents are a thing, or at least part of the reason.

Enjoy being asked to sign a contract—but don't sign it right away! Make sure you know all the details first.

I signed with a traditional publisher and negotiated some better terms for myself, a better royalty rate and some nuances of the audio rights. I went through the contract in detail, knowing a few things about both contracts and sales from previous non-publishing experience. Shortly after signing, the company restructured some of their sales stuff, blah blah blah, and they wanted all authors to sign a contract addendum that promised to make them much more money. I did all the math on my original contract and liked where we'd arrived after negotiating slightly better terms than originally offered. I should have looked much closer at the addendum—I actually lost more than 50% of my royalties because I didn't do the math a second time—it only made me lots of money *if books were purchased through the publisher's website* (who does that!? Nobody goes to the Simon & Shuster website to browse books—they go to a retailer's site). Lesson learned: never take someone's word for it—always double check. I now make about twenty-five cents per book sold, that's waaaay down from about three and a half.

The school of hard knocks is brutal. But at least I can make a bunch on person to person sales, right? Well… almost. My Indie books cost me about five bucks to produce and so I make about ten bucks each sale. My traditional publisher gives a smaller than normal discount. Unless I'm buying in bulk I do not get the market-norm of a 40-50% discount off retail price. I got 30%... plus shipping which is high. Watching your bottom line on details like this is critical—these can easily to slip into the background. My $16.99 book (which cost's less than $4 to print) cost me $11.87 to buy, plus a buck and a half to ship. My books cost me about thirteen and a half dollars apiece. In the end, I felt like Lando Calrissian in Empire Strikes Back: "This deal is getting worse all the time." I wanted to sell them for $15 each, but with event booth fees averaging about $150 plus travel expenses, I'd have to sell more than a hundred books to break even. (This is the reason I always push my Indie titles at the same table… that number is more like 15 books, which is manageable, to sell before I'm in the black.

Always do the math. Always read the fine print. If you have been offered a contract, many literary agents are willing to sign someone for a one-time, quick representation deal (although particularly bad publishers may list a short time limit to sign making authors cave early under the false sense of urgency).

Following are some bad contract clauses that you should be on the lookout for in the event that you are offered a publishing deal. I am not a literary agent nor a publishing professional, so don't take this as legal advice—but *all contracts are negotiable*, and these are contractual aspects that can do you more harm than good, so beware:

•The contract is forever (until you die+70 years)

•Right of first refusal on your next book (unless it's a series)

•The option to match any other publisher's bids on subsequent manuscripts (good luck *ever* getting published elsewhere!)

•A "net" royalty agreement/structure (that thing I signed in the above, tragic tale)

•Any requirement that an author purchases books

•Any requirement that the author purchase a paid service from the publisher

•Author's discount for personal copies is less than 40%

•Any mandatory marketing fees

•A Kill Fee clause

•Clauses that make your contract automatically renew

•Non-compete clauses

•Advances that must be paid back (How about we sign you up for this nice, low-interest loan while we print your book?)

•Royalty rates that drop when sales dip below certain benchmarks

•Indemnity clauses that mean only an author can be sued (and not the publisher)

•Copyright reservation is retained by the publisher and not the author (publisher usually registers them in author's name and then gains specific rights for a specific time period.)

Swimming with Sharks—avoid scams

I know that I've written on this earlier in the book, but it's a good time for a refresher as we delve into the nuts and bolts of launching your Indie book.

Because of targeted marketing and the fact that I am a writer, I am these sorts of companies' ideal consumer (or at least, an ignorant version of me would be.) I get tons of predatory publishing scams popping up in my social media feeds so regularly that they've become white noise.

Once you're familiar with the slimy feeling they induce beneath their thin veneer of accolades, ego stroking, and empty promises, they become easy to spot.

Before the turn of the century many vanity publishers (self-publishers, which is a nuanced difference between Indies and vanity press authors,) began targeting Indie writers with author scams where they represented themselves as legitimate publishers. Some of these included iUniverse, Trafford, Author House and Xlibris. Some more modern examples came along include Tate, Xulon, and to a degree, Book Baby. These companies operate on the premise that they sell products (and false hope) to authors rather than sell books to consumers.

Thankfully, the internet typically reveals the sharks for what they are. Try using your preferred search engine or a service like Preditors and Editors for reviews and horror stories. Even if you know a contracting publisher is legitimate, it may be worth getting perspectives from other authors.

The primary way these companies work is by either steering you or flat out requiring an author to use their services. Legitimate authors pursuing an Indie avenue know that they *ought* to use professional services for editing, cover copy, cover design, etc. and so shady publishers try to sneak under the radar by looking like the real deal while actually making their money off of the *authors* instead of the *books*.

Of course, scammers won't turn down free money from your loved ones, too, and so they *will* still fulfill orders and do the business side of the publishing house—usually while over-inflating the price in order to compensate for the typically low sales that are so common of unknown writes who weren't properly equipped by a legitimate publisher.

Publishing scams typically target first-time authors, most of whom have a manuscript completed (usually as a rough draft) and have begun to ask questions about how to publish. They usually still need editing, typesetting, design, and distribution.

Identifying scammers is relatively easy. (Though they are getting sneakier, a new breed does their research and cold calls authors wanting to represent them at trade shows, etc. But it's the same old song and dance, in the end. Know the following signs and never enter a contract without research. Read my blog for more info on this new breed.)

Ask what the publisher is selling. If it makes claims that you will earn enough money to be a full-time author, or gain fame and accolades, run fast and far. Publishers sell books, not pipe dreams.

If they are pushy and try to get you to commit (and you're not already selling a gazillion copies as an Indie or have millions of reads on Wattpad,) then they are probably a scam.

Publishers get more queries than they can even read—they don't need first and second time authors submitting to them to be happy, and they *certainly* won't chase you down, cold call you, or advertise open submissions on social media. Scammers often have deliberately misleading adverts.

If your book will be priced excessively high, it may be a scam. I do write about proper book pricing elsewhere.

If a publisher charges fees for anything (even upgrades to the "traditional publishing service," flee in a serpentine motion, ducking repeatedly for cover.

The sign I see that is so common is the sale of a "publishing package." Simple rule of thumb is this: whenever someone wants to sell you a "publishing package" of any variety, it's an indicator that *you are the company's primary consumer.*

Publishing should never cost *you*, the author. That's not how this works… not even for debut/break-in authors. You don't pay to get the book in order unless you are an Indie and doing all of the detail work yourself—while the thought that a "package deal" is nice (you can get all of those professional services done for one easy bill,) most of those "services" are so outrageously overpriced that any third grader with rudimentary math skills can tell you it's a bad idea.

You had an idea. *You* did the work to bring your story to life. *You* deserve to make money from your books' sales. Pay to play only works at casinos—and even then, the house always wins. Don't be a book casualty—research everything.

I recommend checking out the list at http://www.sfwa.org/other-resources/for-authors/writer-beware/thumbs-down-publishers/ for further research on the topic and remember to always hold onto your wallet.

Thinking about crowd-funding your novel?

I wanted to touch on the idea of crowdfunding. The big, magic internet thing that makes all of your dreams come true by using the money of others! Are you ready to dream big and shoot for the stars? Well, stop it.

Yeah, yeah. I'm a buzzkill. But it's worth pointing out that realism factors into the equation. Dreaming is great—but crowdfunding a project—any project—takes the same skills and platform that an Indie author ought to be seeking already. If you haven't already successfully harnessed the power of your email list, adverts, and gotten friends and family members to commit to buy then crowdfunding will do nothing but leave you hollowed out with disappointment.

I've stumbled across a few articles on the ole interwebs talking about crowdfunding as it relates to authors and wanted to pass on what I gleaned from them, and from myself who has participated in campaigns as both a backer and a launcher.

#1 (and this is the biggest) Is it really worth it? Count the cost and look at it from a business stand point—do you really think someone will donate to your project based on how you are pitching it and what it is—would you contribute if you didn't know anything but what is listed on your funding page? There's a local guy I know who wanted to be a comedian and talked about his Kickstarter project (needing tens of thousands of dollars) being the "adventure of a lifetime" and how he was going to be big and do recordings and pack out huge shows… his video utterly failed to be funny. He probably watched a bunch of Louis CK on TV or a Made for Netflix comic special and got starry eyed. He bragged about his stage acting experience being a play in high school. He's a 40-year-old burger flipper filming a plea for money from a cell phone. People don't sign onto that kinda thing with their hard-earned cash. It's gotta have a wow factor. And it's got to be real. (As I write this he's launched a new campaign for a million dollars to run for Governor of my home state on a fiercely conservative platform though his only experience is once having a conversation with a congresswoman he thought was great—he didn't realize that she was fiercely liberal). Don't be that guy.

#2, It's going to take more work to secure your backers than trying to generate sales from an Indie book you've published. Think about it like pitching your book a convention or festival: you're going to need good promo materials, a practiced pitch, and a good product (or a realizable dream). If you have that in place now, then you're probably already making money.

#3 It's got to be irresistible and stand out. There's a lot of people using crowd-funding and the market is oversaturated. Can you still do it? Yes. Is it easy to stand out? No... the larger the crowd, the easier it is to get lost in it, at least on the internet.

#4 Don't forget about transparency! You are asking people for cash. They will want to know how it's being spent. There's no such thing as free money and we all want oversight.

#5 Your project will not fund itself! That pesky work thing comes up again. You NEED a platform and buying an email list on Fiverr isn't going to cut it. Reaching people and connecting with them is a MUST in order to get commitments. Most crowdfunding campaigns never reach their goals... just like most Indie books released into the wilds of Amazon never get purchased. If you're not hustling, you're not earning.

#6 Make it worthwhile to backers. Some backers invest solely on the strength of a project's concept; others invest for the rewards that are on offer. This is why it's important to make sure they're alluring. FACT: You're must have good swag and prizes in order to interest backers.

#7 Due Diligence is necessary BEFORE you launch. You need a strategy for sales, but also for the financial management. Do you need $500 (a very small amount by most comparisons) from your campaign to help launch your new 300-page novel? You will need to keep a few things in mind like shipping, production, adverts, etc. Let's look at it quick just to give you an idea of how it's gonna go. It will cost you about $5.00 each to print them and they will probably be a reward for backing at the $15 level or higher (since that's near the book's eventual retail price). Let's say you give away an eBook at the $5 level--that'll cost you about a buck apiece, but there are no shipping factors. Assuming it's part of a series (let's say the third in a trilogy) you can do a larger reward of the whole set for $50. Now for math... target 2x$50 trilogy backers, 20xPaperback purchasers, and 20xEbookers to arrive at 500. those paperbacks will cost you about $3.50 each to ship and the trilogy will cost about $5. Trilogy costs: 15+5=$20 (40 total). Single Paperback: 5+3.50=$8.50 (170 total). EBook: $1 (20 total). That's $230.

But wait. There's more. The earlier shipping costs were just to get the books to your customer... how did you get them? That's right... you have to pay to ship them twice! Good thing it'll be a little cheaper to get those bulk single paperbacks to you. About $5 per trilogy plus only $15 to get them all to you in the first place... lucky dog--you're only down another $25 (totally a $255 investment... we'll assume there are minimal shipping supplies needed and stolen them from your grandmother.) Now we have to figure in the crowd funding fees. 5% is pretty standard, plus credit card fees on top of that (about 8% all-in). That's another $40 out of the $500 resulting in $205 you get to take home from that $500 you fought so hard for. To get to an actual $500, multiply it all by 2.5. You will need x5 Trilogy backers, 50 paperback sponsors, and 50 eBook partners. Also, there is no ad budget built into this—you will need an ad budget!

#8 Remember that there's a deadline. Yes, this can help you get people to jump on board because of the sense of urgency—but also the urgency is very real. Can you really produce the numbers needed on the deadline for commitments? Let's say the above example is a month-long effort... If you simply sold that many books on Amazon you'd make $437.85 $(T/61.35+P/204.50+E/172)$ and have probably stressed less and wouldn't have to the back-end labor associated in my next point.

#9 There's back-end work, too. How much time have you set aside for physically packing, addressing, and shipping your books or other swag? Once the campaign is over, it's still not done. It's just beginning.

The numbers are even more worrying when I look at them in my imaginary sample above. I'm certainly not eager to jump in and attempt a new crowd sourced campaign. I think I'll just take my laptop while I work on my next novel and sell plasma on the side—it might be a more lucrative plan.

How to Do a Good Book Cover

Your book cover is your first impression—if you have any hope of selling the book to someone who doesn't know you then it's got to be a good one. People judge everything by appearance. They say to never judge a book by its cover (or anything else, for that matter,) but we do that *all the time*. You have one of two ways to respond: either change the way our culture thinks (which will take decades and a personal investment numbering in the billions of dollars,) or you can play by the rules already set up by the internal psychology of consumers.

Let me just say a couple things about covers. Your cover is almost as important as what is inside the book—if you don't have the talent to create an amazing cover, don't fake it, skimp, or settle for something that doesn't really pop. I waited almost 3 years to publish my nonfiction book because I wasn't happy with any possible cover art pieces. Once I found what I'd always envisioned and made it happen that book became my bestseller. A cover is your first and best marketing tool, and *most people* do a crap job at it. I'm not mincing words here. Three quarters of all the Indie book submissions I receive for my review service have covers that are absolute garbage. (I'm loathe to admit that one of my early covers ended up on an award site for "bad covers" which prompted me to learn about this. I then commissioned an artist to redo my cover with certain thematic elements and my sales took off.)

You should know that there are some industry standards for covers that you ought to abide by. Most of these are touched on if you use the tools available in Createspace's cover creator, but not all of them. For instance, Createspace and most other Indie presses will put a bar code on your cover graphic, but they will not automatically put the price next to that UPC code—some book buyers, services, and stores will not carry a book that does not have one (though many will) because that is considered an industry standard. Your cover artist will need to manually put that that onto your artwork if you want it included (just be warned that future price changes won't be reflected on your cover art and so you will need to keep your artwork current and change this if necessary which could incur charges depending on how you've set up your printing.

Below are the kinds or cover elements that make them absolute garbage (no visible appeal—or worse, make people want to *avoid* your book).

•A tightly cropped image/extreme close-up meant to distract from the fact that an author couldn't find/commission artwork that *is* relevant to a story… or an image resized with improper aspect ratio (making it squished)

•Characters, faces, or CG images that look they come from a late 90s video game (or really anything meant for 3D but represented in 2D)

•Bad fonts (I'm looking at you Papyrus)

•No texture or depth to text overlays

•Looks like it was assembled in MS Paint

•Bad photo-manipulation

•Unreadable and/or crowded text or improperly placed text

•Bad image blending techniques (superimposed pieces look like a 1970s green screen, etc.)

•Artwork that looks like it belongs on a refrigerator rather than a book cover (unless it's a kids' picture book)

•Spelling errors

•Design is either too simple or too complex (if a cover has just text on a blank background, *or* it suffers from too many inserted graphic elements or is too busy the book becomes unappealing— it's the visual equivalent of a cover blurb that is either too long or too short)

•Clashing art techniques (like *pencil* drawings overlaid on a stock-image *photo*)

•Rampant abuse of opacity/transparency overlays

•…and my ultimate pet peeve that I see *all the time*: a stock image scenery photo with text overlay (like seriously, this is about 40% of all the *bad books* that I see and accounts for most people who put zero effort into this critically important marketing tool.) The only real exceptions to this are poetry books, some kinds of memoirs, or books about landscaping.

Some of the generally recognized industry standards that you should be aware of are

• Human readable BISAC code

• All text is easily readable at full size *and* as a thumbnail

• Spine includes author name, title, and publisher info

• Human readable ISBN on back cover

• Bar code on back cover with 13-digit ISBN

There are many services on the internet or individual freelancers willing to help with a book cover—but be sure to ask for examples of work before you commit money or enter into a contract for the work. There many other reputable services available online. For a DIY cover design, try to avoid the above list of bad cover elements if you are committed to voyaging ahead with your copy of Photoshop or similar program. For a DIY designer, your biggest concern will be securing rights to quality artwork to merge into your greater cover design.

Where to get Art for your DIY Cover

For many DIY authors who have either a familiarity with software and aspects of design, access to great templates for covers, or just want to try their own hand making covers, knowing where to get license free artwork is beneficial.

One quick caveat on cover art, numerous people have made many, many *really* bad book covers. Good enough to satisfy doesn't cut it. This is one more area where the failure of Indies (or their apathy towards the subject) has made the term "self-published" synonymous with "crap." Please don't take a dump on the book pile before you add to it. If you are committed to releasing your DIY cover into the wild, please make sure that it doesn't reflect poorly upon Indies as a whole. There are many services that will gladly contract with you to design the cover you have in mind (just check their portfolio, first, to make sure he or she isn't some fly-by night with a demo copy of Photoshop striking out with no more skill than the next guy.) If you see multiple images that you'd love merged into your ideal graphic but don't have the skill to seamlessly integrate them, please don't go at it alone.

There are many places to acquire stock images for use in your covers:

http://www.istockphoto.com   and http://www.shutterstock.com are both highly recommended. I have memberships at both and use them often. I have also been a member of http://www.deviantart.com for many years. Its forum has been a mostly fruitful place for me to hire professional illustrators for a variety of writing-related commissions.

For the ultimate in DIY on the cheap you can search for free images at sources that aggregate CC0 license stock images. Please use *these places* and not Google Image Search. A Google Image search will also show copyrighted images and you can quickly find yourself in legal trouble for infringement—an author who willfully infringes on the copyright of someone else (this is basically plagiarism) will find little support from the community at large.

CC0 stands for Creative Commons Zero. Under the terms of the license, all images may be used, displayed, or modified freely for *personal or commercial* use. The only stipulation is that identifiable faces should not be used in potentially offensive ways (like book covers for erotica). No attribution is needed. (More here: https://creativecommons.org/publicdomain/zero/1.0/)

My favorite site tops this list, others follow.

> https://pixabay.com
> https://www.pexels.com/
> http://unsplash.com/
> http://www.publicdomainpictures.net/
> http://publicdomainarchive.com/
> http://littlevisuals.co/
> http://pickupimage.com/
> http://www.pdpics.com/
> https://stocksnap.io/
> http://skitterphoto.com/

Picking your cover art and design motifs are one thing, but remember the practical things, too. Your spine's thickness, and whether your pages are white or crème (they have different thicknesses when added up,) will depend upon exactly how many pages are in your book. Rather than do all of the math, I'd recommend searching online for a "book cover calculator" that will adjust your spine width for you and give you a template to design over with proper bleed and trim edges. Both Createspace and Ingramspark have these features built into their creation wizards and allow users to upload their own files for quality proofing by their own experts (mostly Skynet computers who gained sentience.)

Because of the large file sizes and opportunities to constantly tweak, change, or mess up, I recommend saving often, and save in multiple formats. I always save any final WIP twice. One that I intend to upload as a Photoshop PDF with all layers merged together and at 300DPI (always work in 300DPI—you can always lose quality, but never gain it) and an original with layers intact. Some publishers have maximum file sizes meant to keep their servers from imploding; merging the layers helps bring that size down significantly.

When you're done, make sure to get a physical proof ordered by your printer. Oftentimes colors will represent as darker or lighter once ink hits the paper. I intentionally upgrade the vibrancy of my covers so that they pop more. Printed covers tend to either look faded or darker than they do on the screen.

If you're reluctant to give it a go or realize that you need a high-quality cover and don't possess the highly advanced skillset needed to do so, you can get some very good covers at very reasonable prices at https://selfpubbookcovers.com/ (in the $50-$150 price range.)

Happy designing, and don't feel bad if you get unhappy results. I've scrapped pieces that I didn't love... and my biggest publishing regrets come from using artwork that wasn't quite ready for the world to see. Don't publish unfinished art or unedited stories. The world won't thank you for *not* doing that... but it *will* ridicule you if you ignore that advice.

Formatting your Book's Interior

I have seen many different format designs for pages. There is very little by way of right and wrong when it comes to font, letter size, margins, etc. There is not a one-size fits all motif. There are some industry standards, however, and some things that just make sense.

I write about size of books elsewhere, but book dimensions are a tricky thing. Many people prefer a 6x9 for all books—I hate 6x9 unless I'm reading nonfiction... then I think it's the perfect size. I prefer a 5.5x8.5 in fact or even a 5x8. That's all just personal preferences, though.

Font choice also ranges greatly but I recommend standard fonts like Times New Roman or Courier and an approximate size somewhere between 11 and 14, depending on the genre and audience. Line spacing is very important as well. Double spacing is *much* too large, 1.5 is better, and 1.15 is my preference (for fiction, anyway,) and 1.0 is much too crowded and strains the eyes.

Margins are very important. One inch is pretty common, but leaves more whitespace at the edges than many readers care for, unless the book is a 6x9 or larger. Half-inch is better for fiction if the trim size is less than 6x9. Gutter margins are another thing you will need to keep in mind.

What the heck are gutter margins you ask? When your book is bound, the left-hand side of the recto page (and right hand of the verso) needs extra space to account for the spine of the book and where the thick sheaf of paper is glued together at its binding. If you don't create a gutter margin your text will run off into oblivion (especially if your margins are tight). It's not nearly as difficult as it sounds. Simply put, a gutter margin is an additional amount of space your word processing software will add to the binding side to keep the margins correct. The size of your gutter margins depends upon the overall page count of your book. Createspace recommends the following gutter sizes:

24-50 pages	.375"
151-400 pages	.75"
400-600 pages	.875"
+600 pages	1.0"

Formatting might sound like a big headache when you just want to write (and there are plenty of people who will do all your formatting for a fee,) but it really is critical to get this right. It's important and there are industry standards for a reason. Poor formatting hastens eye fatigue and makes readers quit, good formatting helps salability and profitability.

At the end of the day, reducing whitespace (within reason) means fewer pages and that means extra money earned per book sold. But if the layout looks bad with text too small, too large, too squished, or bad margins, the interior looks unprofessional and thus unappealing—that turns people off from buying it. Those same things cause the eyes and minds of the people who *do* read it to grow weary more quickly making them likely to put the book down (the opposite of "a page-turner.") Time spent tweaking formats can have a broad, positive impact down the road on the reader's side.

The Independent Book Publishers Association lists a number of generally recognized industry standards on their website: http://www.ibpa-online.org/page/standardschecklist (you can check out their list of standards for covers as well). These standards include:

•Professional appearance

•Appropriate, easily readable font for body of text
•Consistent headers and footers
•Proper punctuation usage (em dash, hyphens, etc.)
•Appropriate margins
•Strategic trim size

The interior file should also include the following elements in addition to the text of the story:

•Half-Title page (has just the title of the book on the first page... this page is optional)
•Title Page to include title/subtitle of book, author(s)/editors, illustrators, publisher, and location. The Title and Half-Title pages should always be on the right-hand side (recto) pages
•Copyright page (should be on left-hand [verso] page following Title Page,) that includes copyright date and holder, copyright notice, edition information, Library of Congress info, publisher info, ISBN, title, author, design credits, waivers, and disclaimers
•Optional Dedication
•Optional Table of Contents
•Optional Acknowledgements page, including possible back matter for footnotes, endnotes, and formally credited citations
•About the Author (this may appear in front matter, back matter, or on the jacket/rear cover)

EBook formatting is slightly different. When creating an eBook from a paperback (if you are using Createspace) you can automatically push the file from Createspace to Kindle/KDP and the conversion will take place automatically for you. This means that as long as you did it correctly for the paperback the eBook should be fine. Smashwords, however (which you should definitely use) has their own formatting procedures which are perhaps a little more difficult to nail down correctly (things like hyperlinks within the text and specific formatting methods for the Table of Contents, front matter, back matter, etc.) the end result is actually a more powerful book and one that is available on more platforms. While some people don't bother with Smashwords because of the added difficulty and the fact that the sales via

Smashwords pale in comparison to Amazon, it is worth it for a variety of other reasons. Smashwords pushes the book to Kobo, iBook's, B&N, and bunch of other places where users shop; the primary reason I like it, though, is the ease of setting up coupons to give discounts or free copies to people like reviewers, press, con attendees, etc. Smashwords and other eBook specific hosting/publishing outlets will have their own specific guidelines on how to format, prepare, and submit files.

Getting your back-cover matter done right

A book's cover must be good. It's got to engage and set a hook. Essentially, the front cover has to make them want to pick the book up; the back-cover matter has to keep it in their hand. It's really a one-two punch that makes them want to buy your book. It's their first peek at what you have and it's your responsibility, as an author, to keep them there.

Think of your book like a house. Even with a pristine interior, if the outside is a dump they won't want to look inside—that's the cover. A blurb is their peek through the door or window; if there's a dead hooker lying on the floor, they probably won't want to go in—don't let your back cover look trashed or sloppy. Purchasing your book is a reader's agreement live inside this house for a while. Nobody wants to stay in a meth-house with dead prostitute roommates, no matter how cheap that Airbnb might be… never again.

A lot of Indie writers make the mistake of flying by the seat of their pants on the back cover (myself included). It's easy to look at it flippantly and think *dang, I just wrote 100,000 +/- words… another 200 words is a cakewalk*. It is not. These might be the most difficult to write well and might be your most important. You have one short page worth of text to convince someone to take this book home—it's got to be the best page. As with most Indies, this might also be the text you have at the top of your book description on Amazon, Goodreads, B&N, Smashwords, etc. It will be your primary ad copy so do it right.

While I write both nonfiction and fiction, I'm concentrating my cover content advice on fiction. Much applies to both types.

What should be on my back cover?

Space is limited, so remember that this is expensive real estate and everything has to work perfectly. What *goes on* your back cover may be as important as what you are sure to *leave off*! If you have an endorsement, it had better be a good one—someone recognized as a bona fide expert or name in the genre… anything less may be a waste of space. Ensure that your short bio is written tightly and includes a photo, but make it a quality headshot that is cropped neatly. A shortlist of things on your rear would include 1. Blurb/text 2. Small photo 3. Short Bio 4. One-line Hook (sometimes called a logline), single-sentence elevator pitch, or gripping headline 5. Optional endorsement.

Back cover elements of the primary text:

The above elements are a pretty good rule of thumb—but how do you write the actual text? Your content should be similar to the story overview pieces you might have included in a query letter to prospective literary agents or publishers. A good formula for this is to 1. introduce your characters (and any brief elements that are necessary to the environment—don't build a world here or focus on the setting, but if it's in the 1800's or an alien planet, you might mention it). 2. Describe the central conflict they face and 3. highlight the stakes. Ask the question what will happen if your protagonists fail.

There are many approaches to take and many writers swear by certain elements/formulas. Here are a few elements you may want to highlight

•keep the book "at a glance friendly." If it looks overwhelming to a casual reader, they probably won't wade into the text with much sincerity.
•provoke emotions or entice readers with questions or promises
•use a rhythm and voice that sets a tone. Think of the book as a movie and the back cover like a movie trailer—you have only a few short sentences to suck them in. Build a cadence and hook them.

•focus on what your book is about, not what happens in its pages. You aren't summarizing the plot; you are crafting a hook to the story at large

One formula you might like is proposed by author and editor Victoria Mixon (victoriamixon.com) and goes like this: **When [*identity*] [*protagonist name*] [*does something*], [*something happens*]. Now, with [*time limit/restrictions*], [*protagonist*] must [*do something brave*] to [*accomplish great achievement*]/ or [*sacrifice high stakes*].**

Other things to keep in mind:

•The font should be readable and sized appropriately. Pick a color that stands out and is easy to read. I've erred here before and quickly made corrections. Sometimes it doesn't look as nice on paper as it does on a screen; always purchase a galley copy to double check how it looks in print.

•Keep the blurb on the shorter side—you want it succinct. Think about the success of Twitter: the shorter something is, the more likely it is to be read.

•Typos and grammar or style errors are a sure giveaway to a reader that the book was pushed out too early. I've found some in my own books and I always go back and fix them ASAP... sometimes things get missed by editors, but it creates a huge obstacle to selling people your book. Thanks to POD, you can fix most of these as they arise, but it's a better plan to avoid them in the first place.

•Pick a consistent voice for your text and think about your audience before you put pen to paper. If the writing comes off as pretentious or juvenile you will probably alienate readers (even if you are targeting pretentious or juvenile readers.) Some voices work, some don't. Give voicing some thought *before* you write it so you can color it appropriately.

If you want to delve into this topic further, I would recommend this blog:
https://www.thebookdesigner.com/2013/05/casey-demchak-back-cover-copy/

Getting and Using Author Central

Amazon.com is big. Reeeeaallly big—and they account for more than 60% of all other sales combined for most Indie authors. That said, they want you to succeed (albeit, just so they can make a profit off of you, but that's how business works.) Amazon wants you to do well so that they can get their cut (which is why they have virtually zero interest in making your *Createspace* store a convenient place to shop for customers who will simply order via the regular Amazon system instead, resulting in more cash for the king.) To help you do better, Amazon has equipped authors with this nifty tool called Author Central. You can log in or sign up for it at: http://www.authorcentral.com/

If you've read my Indie Roadmap, you will see that the list has a special entry for getting into Author Central. You can use this in lieu of a personal website, but it should probably have both and mirror the same kind of content.

Author Central allows you to connect with readers by creating a profile which will be cross-loaded into all of your books' sales pages. It's a good place to put a bio, some catchy images, and even video. Perhaps one good feature that is often overlooked is the Events option where you can list upcoming appearances such as conventions, fairs, festivals, and signings. Another feature, if you have a regular blog, is something called RSS feeds. I specifically chose hosting my blog with WordPress because of the RSS feature. I'm no tech guru, and you may need to turn over a few more stones to properly utilize this option, but it takes the content from my blog and reposts it on my Author Central profile so that it is automatically updated with new content every time I post (which is several times per week) … I do this for my Goodreads account as well. You can also link your social media accounts to your Author Central so make sure to do that—it is always a good idea to be connected to your readers—more so now than ever before. Readers want more than a good story: they want relationships with good storytellers!

According to Amazon, getting an account is this easy:

> Visit https://authorcentral.amazon.com/ and click **Join Now**.

> Enter your e-mail address and password and click **Sign in using our secure server**.

> If you have an Amazon.com account, sign in with the e-mail address and password you use on that account.

> If you do not have an existing Amazon.com account, select **No, I am a new customer**. You will be prompted to enter the necessary information.

> Read the Author Central's Terms and Conditions, and then click **Agree** to accept them.

> Enter the name your books are written under. A list of possible book matches appears.

> Select any one of your books. If your book is not in the list, you can search for it by title or ISBN. The book you select must be available for purchase on the Amazon.com website to use this…

> When you receive the confirmation e-mail, confirm your e-mail address and identity.

That really is about the gist of it. It's streamlined, easy to use, and is a convenient way to put your greater work in front of shoppers who might want to learn more about an author or check out his or her backlist.

Once you are able to fill out the biography (after step 6) you should remember a few things: write in the third person; use your writing style to show readers your personality; use the bio to establish your credibility; keep it clean, appealing, and readable—you only have a couple paragraphs to "sell yourself," so be neither boring, nor too short. Also of note is that you can't use any html or even bold or italic fonts in this bio—words only... but you're a writer, right? So write.

Something else I learned is that authors should be sure to sign up for Author Central accounts in *both* the US market *and* the UK market. They don't necessarily mirror each other, but a little copy and pasting can fix that. You can find the UK version at https://authorcentral.amazon.co.uk

Setting the Price of Your Book

This is a pretty tricky thing—and it's more difficult than you might think and it is. Quite honestly, it's something I've always struggled with.

Many smaller presses have what feels like outrageously inflated prices... sometimes that's true, but sometimes that's my background context wreaking havoc with my economic sense. I grew reading at a young age and often bought books from library sales, used book bins, and mass market copies off the shelf of my local drug store; if a book was anywhere close to $20 it had to be a hardcover novel that just released. In the back of my mind I'm still thinking that all paperbacks ought to be $5.99, just like my dad thinks a soda ought to cost a nickel and we should crack open a fire hydrant if we want to cool down on a summer day.

Of course, it's ridiculous to live in the past and to base your books' prices on such old models... even if you print copies of your book in bulk to resell, you're going to have paid around $5.99 (give or take a dollar) per unit just to have them printed and shipped to you. I'm constantly tweaking my prices, looking at the issue, and realizing that many readers are used to paying $12-15 for a new book. Their metric is different than the ancient days I grew up in; $12.99 is the new $5.99... people who are interested in my books at signings seldom balk at an approximate $15 price tag given the size and weight of the book they're holding.

But that's not to say that you should price all your books at $15. You've got to decide a few things with your pricing: 1. What is your goal/purpose in writing, 2. Are you communicating true value with your book, and 3. Is your price market feasible.

Are you in this to make some money or are you willing to make less money so that more people will be able to buy your book based on a low price? Many writers (myself included) are more interested in having readers and building a solid fandom than they are with making money. This may change at some point, but at least for now I am just trying to break even with my book sales. If you are trying to price your book so cheaply that people can't hardly refuse to buy it (trust me—many will still refuse,) then you might be limiting your books potential market feasibility.

If you set your book price too low, you risk communicating that your writing has low value/worth… sometimes low-cost things are "cheap" and oftentimes free things aren't worth the $0.00 price tag. If you want people to buy-in and take you seriously as a writer, do two things. 1. Make sure that the book is indeed good (honest reviews from beta readers, your book was edited well, it's not a rip-off of some other story). 2. Don't give away something that has real value/cost (unless it's a specific promo tactic with a time-limit).

You want to make sure that your book can enter mainstream distribution and is feasible. Regardless of whether or not *you* would give away your book, resellers and bookstores *do not feel the same way*. If your book costs $5 to manufacture and you want to sell it for $7.50, it will not be available on Amazon and bookstores won't sell it—there is no margin for them to mark it up and sell it. You could buy copies and store them and then enter them into distribution, but for a bookstore to carry it, they demand certain wholesale prices (they will sell the book at $7.50, but will only pay $3.37 per copy which you will have about $7 invested into at the end of the day (after production and shipping costs) plus another dollar or more that it will cost you if the book is returned to clear space for new books—that $7.50 book costs you about $8 or more at that point—it's just not feasible to lose $5 on every book that you "sell" (wholesale cost versus your actual cost). You've got to take that into consideration when looking at the pricing. Thankfully, there are some handy built-in guides within Createspace and Ingramspark that will help you, and some general recommendations in this article.

I used to sell my fiction at a discount at conventions for a slightly reduced price... (my $16.95 book sold for $15, a nice and simple round number.) At the end of the sale, even if I discount my book to $15, I still had to pay sales tax on that. If I am invested into the book for $6 and take $15 per book, my profit isn't $9. Sales tax is about $1.50, making my profit $7.50, and another $0.50 for a credit card fee at 3% (figures are rounded and approximate.) You can see how nickels and dimes hemorrhage out of a sale. You're only taking home $7 off of that $17 book, and you still have to pay for a booth/table fee that is common to most conventions. This same book gets worse numbers if you're published through a small press and your author discount is something like 20-40% off retail rather than the actual production cost. (By the above metric, before I pay for my booth fees I've lost about $2 for every book sold if I bought it from my traditional publisher at a 20% discount. Bleeding. Money.)

The solution is to be smart; don't flush your wallet down the toilet. If I sell my 350-page fantasy novel that costs me about $5 shipped for $16.99 and then add tax (Square does this nicely for you in their app—more on that later,) then the consumer pays their tax and you pay about .50 in banking fees, netting you about 11.50 (more, actually, but you need to keep that portion set aside to pay taxes at the end of the year).

I know... this seems like math overload and you just want to write stories, right? Following is some good nuts and bolts info on how to set a price point. (There is as much danger in setting a price too low as there is in setting it too high... although, setting it too low has a built in lowest-price threshold since it can't go into distribution if it's too low.)

Most average sized (300-400 page) trade paperbacks fall into the 13.95-17.95 price range. Of course, you should still visit a few bookstores and find books similar to genre before landing on a reasonable price. Don't fall prey to the thought that someone will buy *your* YA dystopia instead of the newest *Maze Runner* because yours is $2 cheaper. Also, readers buy consumable content—you have to have a good story and convince them of it. It's more likely, if you do that, that they will buy *both* rather than picking between titles. (If you tried to outprice the professionals and they buy both, you've just lost money you shouldn't have and undersold/devalued yourself). Avid readers are more *both/and* than they are *either/or*.

The best place to find your low-price threshold will be via the most expensive distributor you plan to use. I am an advocate of using both Createspace and Ingramspark for a variety of reasons written about elsewhere. The latter is slightly more expensive to both print and distribute, but it helps you determine what your lowest price will be after allowing for all costs, fees, and wholesaler discounts. (Use most expensive distributor's production cost at a price set that also covers the return shipping costs allowing you to break even.)

Thinking about it in these terms is cold and calculating, but it's a *must* to establish pricing boundaries. However, don't think about it *only* in these terms. Think about it also from the value readers get and the investment of your precious time.

…hold your horses… you can't sell it for $100, either. You have to find a balance, like all things in life, but feel free to find the best path that works for you.

As far as eBook pricing goes, all the same ideas still apply, but the costs are different and more relative to bandwidth and electronic gobbledygook that few humans understand or care about (it's less real to us on this side of the internet.) Luckily there is a general consensus and rough guide for pricing based on word length:

$0.99 Flash Short-stories: Under 3K

$1.99 Short-stories: 3-7K

$2.99 Novelette Stories: 7-15K

$3.99 Novella Short-stories: 15-35K

$4.99 Short Novels: 35-50K

$5.99 Mid-sized Novels 50-70K

$6.99 Large Novels: 70-140K

Of course, all of these are just suggested guidelines. If you're either famous or unknown, these rules go straight out the window with great frequency. Besides, I'm just an author/blogger who learned a few things via the school of hard knocks—what do I know, anyway? Find what works for you—and if something isn't clicking, change it!

Amazon/Createspace's Primary Weakness and How to Get Around It

If you've been writing for any length of time then hopefully you've been doing some promotion in order to sell your book… or in the absence of sales, get your book read by an audience. Why else would you write and then publish as an Indie unless you want to be read?

I've advocated using Createspace as an avenue to get published for no upfront costs… I'm still baffled by the services advertising for paid "publishing packages." Then again, every year there is a new crop of starry-eyed writers hoping to break out as the next great author, but doesn't yet know the ropes.

Createspace pushes straight to Amazon and is a totally free, mostly automated system. Amazon accounts for about 70% of the sales for Indie published books. If you are going to sell online, then you MUST be on Amazon, and there is no easier and more efficient way to do this than by harnessing the power of Createspace.

So, where's the weakness? If your goal is to be carried on bookshelves at local or chain bookstores you will find the weakness in their distribution system. The problem is two-fold. Firstly, they are a victim of their own success. Amazon is viewed as a direct competitor to local bookstores and so many won't ever purchase books put out by Createspace. They have a bias—but would overlook it if a customer was in the store making a request… it won't make the shelf, though, because the wholesale discount is only 40%, which is less than the normal discount of 55% that stores want.

But Createspace distributes through Ingram, the largest network there is—Ingram's got everyone, right? Well, yes... but there is something called Returnability... bookstores can't sell back any unpurchased items if they came from Createspace. And there's the rub... most brick and mortars WILL NOT carry a title without the option of returning old stock—it assumes too much risk on the store's part. More than prejudice against Amazon, this keeps you off most brick and mortar shelves.

That's a problem for many... however, there is a way to get your title carried in Ingram AND have returnability... use Ingramspark. I will talk about it more in a future article—but the take away for now is this: Createspace alone will rarely be sufficient to get your happy, shiny books onto the shelves down the street, net you to book signings and promo events at chain stores, etc.

I recommended using both Amazon's Createspace AND Ingramspark in order to get the best of both worlds. It's more work, but adds a huge level of credibility to you as an author.

Firstly, it's important to clarify your goals with publishing. Hardly any physical bookstore will carry a title they can't return (barring some personal connection or a consignment program,) as a matter of principle. *But maybe that's not one of your goals.* Stores would likely still order a Createspace title if a customer special ordered it... Createspace DOES utilize the Ingram catalogue—they just have a no returns policy. If you don't care about being represented on an actual bookshelf, maybe this isn't important to you and foregoing it might even save you a couple bucks (there is a $50 setup fee per title, plus you must purchase/provide an ISBN separately—you can get a coupon for free setup, but you will have to buy an ISBN).

Ingramspark's setup is not nearly as user friendly as Createspace and most new users will have trouble with it. You must be sure to setup your pricing correctly and setup the returnability options properly or else you've just bungled the reasons for undertaking this added work. You should also go into your Createspace settings and make sure to turn off the Expanded Distribution options in the CS dashboard or else bookstores you approach about carrying your titles might get confused and decide not to order because of multiple listings in their catalogue each at different rates. Turning this off circumvents any anti-Amazon prejudice.

While there are fees for Ingramspark, there are ways to get your title setup for almost nothing. When I entered my Ingramspark titles I used a coupon code and got the setup fees waived. I utilized a highly reviewed ISBN service to get ISBNs for less than ten bucks (I used http://www.epubbud.com). Because I do my own art and I already had the formatted files prepared and could convert them to the necessary format (PDF,) I had no other expenses. It literally cost me only $9 to get my title available at Ingramspark with full returnability. Because I go to chain stores to do signings (and stores like Barnes and Nobles like to carry a few extras for their inventory—but won't order if they can't return,) having control over the pricing options, royalty/discount ratios, and returnability are absolutely crucial to me.

I make the vast majority of my sales through Amazon (the Createspace version of my book). I get a better royalty through Amazon than through Ingramspark—especially since I'm using Ingram as my wholesale option. A person COULD funnel it all through Ingramspark if they wanted, but the royalties go down slightly and you lose the ability to utilize things like Kindle Unlimited for promotions… then again maybe that's not a part of your plan.

Hopefully you've picked up on the key element to this post: if you are an Indie, you can't just release a book into the wild and hope it survives and thrives—you've got to have a plan. Luckily, it's never too late to develop one. If you need help, connect with some other authors and seek advice.

For more reading, here are a few great posts with more details on utilizing Ingramspark for Indies:

http://www.newshelves.com/2016/05/21/why-you-need-lightning-source-and-createspace/
http://selfpublishingadvice.org/watchdog-ingram-spark-vs-createspace-for-self-publishing-print-books/
http://selfpublishingadvice.org/how-to-use-createspace-and-ingram-spark-together/

How Do I Get My Book on Audible?

A lot of newer authors, or those who just don't know, think that being on Audible or having an audiobook is a huge hassle or is very expensive… while it *can* be the case—it doesn't need to be.

If you have the right skillset or a little guidance (such as this book,) then you can take your published work and have it put into print as a paperback for absolutely no cost. You can also have it converted for absolutely NOTHING into a Kindle eBook (and it will be available also on nook, kobo, apple, etc. via other services.) Finally, an option exists to do the same for an audiobook. You might think that you must own high-end audio recording equipment to do it for free—THAT IS NOT THE CASE!

I'll level with you early. I *do* have some recording equipment and all the software necessary as part of my bygone music-making days. Equipment is something necessary for an audio producer: the person who records, mixes, masters, and encodes the sound files that make up your audiobook: they transcribe your written piece into audio. That person *can be you* if you desire (and possess the equipment and skillset,) but it doesn't have to be you in order to have your audio book made at no cost.

So, here's how it works: once your book is listed on Amazon.com through Createspace, click the "make eBook" tab in the production guide for your book—this will send your files to Kindle. Many users of eBooks find audiobooks directly through the books they've downloaded, so don't skip the eBook (if your goal was to get read, this opens many new doors). Once that is done, go to the site where audiobooks are made: acx.com… it stands for Audible Creation eXchange.

The trick to keeping entry costs down to nothing is to understand that you can opt for a commission split with a recording engineer. This gives him or her a vested interest in your audiobooks. It allows them, without any pay upfront, to create your audiobook and receive 50% of your earned royalties on the book's audio format (only the audio—which they will pour many hours of skilled labor into.) It makes them a 50/50 partner for this one product only.

Here's how it works:

Audible.com will host your files and do the listing/distribution of the files. They get their cut off the top and earn a whopping 60% of the royalties (I know! That's a lot—but it's their game. You can either take your ball and go home, or let them help you sell your stories—and remember, you don't have to put *any effort* into your audiobook once you find an audio producer, so saying no might cost you money you didn't even realize you could be making.

Select the commission split option and follow the guide. Tell them what you're looking, even note which kind of voice you're looking for (gender, accent, etc.) and copy/paste a script for narration which the engineers will read as an audition. Over a course of a few weeks several creators might send in auditions.

Pick the one you like best, and then let them do the work! This does take some time, but it's all labor that you won't have to perform or pay for with this option.

The main thing you *would* need to do is watch the sales through the tracking console (it's the same kind of format as Amazon/Createspace and Kindle... the only difference is that it doesn't tell you immediately what your earnings are because of their sliding scale. (As a service, Audible has three different rates which they pay out at depending on the buyer's subscription rate, how many books they've gotten this month, or if they aren't a subscribing customer.)

Here's a great article which lists a few details I didn't go into (like profit rates, how amazon decides to price your audiobook, etc.) that might be of interest to some.

http://authormarketinginstitute.com/how-acx-earnings-work/

Keys to Making People Excited About Your Book

People ask me all the time, "Which book that you wrote is your favorite?" That's difficult to answer, but honestly, it's typically whichever book I'm currently working on. But the *correct* answer is the *right* answer. The real answer isn't the title of one of your books; it's enthusiasm. *You need to be excited about your stories.* If you are not, no one else will be either. Here are some keys to getting other people excited for your books.

Excitement. You've got to be excited about your book(s)—not just the fact that *you* wrote it, but it has got to genuinely *be a book you would buy.* To test this, you've got to let it simmer... once your final draft is done, let it sit a few months in a drawer or on a hard drive... go do something else, start a new book, even... then come back and read it with fresh eyes. If it doesn't excite you, then it's time to reevaluate the book (even a final draft isn't necessarily a final draft) and not every book needs to be published. I have one on my hard-drive that excites me in theory, but needs such a total rewrite that I might never get around to it. It's okay to let it go.

Great Cover Copy. Your blurb/elevator pitch has to be on point. I write about this elsewhere with sample formulas. Aside from your opening page, this is your opportunity to set a killer hook. An amazing tagline is also great tool (a one sentence summary).

Amazing First Page. What comes up when you click Amazon's Look Inside feature—or what does a reader do when you put a book in his or her hand (besides read the cover copy)? People default to the first page. Give them some irresistible bait. Don't be hokey, cheesy, or overly gimmicky. *Be good.* Incidentally, this is also a critically important piece for literary agents who get deluged with reading requests every day.

Superb Cover Art. Maybe this should've been higher on the list since it's practically sequential, but the cover is the very first thing a reader sees. If it reeks of sub-par quality or feels amateurish the reader isn't likely to be as receptive to your enthusiasm and might not even bother reading the cover copy.

Know Your Reader. People are meant to exist in community, so find out where your readers are and what they like—engage them on familiar ground. I write mostly SF/F so there is little surprise that I do well at comic conventions. If you write something similar to Chicken Soup For the Soul, a scrapbooking or quilting club is a great place to talk about your book and engage readers. I would do terribly at a historical society meeting, but a nonfiction author who writes on regional interests could do well. Identify your target audience... go to your target audience.

As much as I wish there was some kind of magic bullet to make your book irresistible to consumers, there is not. No special formulas or methods exist, just pure, unadulterated hard work, enthusiasm, ability to sell, and drive to keep promoting your book. When your energy runs low, take a breather. If it doesn't come back, fake it. Push through until something breaks—if your book is good and if you're present with your prime target audience, persistence will always rule over resistance.

Be tenacious. Be excited. You've got this.

I Need Reviews—Where Can I find Reviewers?

First and foremost, hit up any person you can think of that has read your book. Offer free copies to legitimate reviewers, etc. Of course, this begs the question, "Where do I find legitimate reviewers?" Equally important is how to do that without breaking the bank… especially, since you will usually need to pay for a copy of the book for him or her to read.

Finding reviewers might be the hardest part. There are a few databases online that list reviewers with links to their sites and the genres that they actively review. One that I often use is The Indie View; it's been around since 2010 and has 381 reviewers listed. Their website belongs in your bookmarks tab: http://www.theindieview.com/indie-reviewers/
        Here are another two worthwhile directories:
http://buggin4bookblogs.com/
https://bookbloggerdirectory.wordpress.com/

There are many lists out there that will help you find reviewers, but keep in mind that they will each have their own submissions guidelines, likes, and dislikes. I run my own service as well and I am particular about what I see submitted.

Few things in my inbox irk me more than a form letter that was obviously blanket-emailed to every email address a person could find—even worse, however, are people who pay such little attention to guidelines that they write nasty responses back after a rejection. Don't add stupidity to ignorance. If you submit to a book reviewer, please remember that there is a real person on the other end of the email.

Review services and sites are great. However, your first and best reviews come from those closest to you. If *they* won't leave a good review, you might need to rethink publishing.

Best Ways to Query For a Book Review

Like all Indie authors I am pretty desperate for book reviews—we can never have enough. It's a fact of the system and a way of life: books with no reviews (or a lack of any recent ones,) fall to the bottom of the proverbial barrel and will not be seen by the target audience. This could be your new favorite, top pick of all time, but un-reviewed books remain undiscovered by new readers (this is why it's so important to leave glowing reviews for titles you enjoyed).

Like all authors I've asked all my family and friends first... then onto tier two. Out of about 900 Facebook friends I got something like 5 reviews (I know, that's about 1/2% of my people.) It's not that I've been a terrible person or that people don't want to help me—authors should understand that 1/2-1% is a pretty typical figure... beyond single digits is astronomical. Of those friends *who did* leave a review, each of them were asked specifically and separately—no boiler-plate copy+paste plea. People want that kind of attention (it's a life lesson more so than just something that applies to the review-o-sphere.)

Gisela Hausmann, an Amazon top reviewer (yes, they rank even that sort of thing,) wrote a brief advice column in the Huffington Post. Here is a summation of her advice on things to avoid doing:

> Don't tailor a template. Use your own words. You're a writer, right? So write. Top reviewers get lots of requests; they recognize templates and it tells reviewers the requester is lazy.

> Make a case for your book. They want something different, not something similar to XYZ.

Avoid writing Me-Mail. Remove as many personal pronouns as possible. Drop "I wrote a book about..." in favor of "You'll love my books..."

Don't waste words. Keep it around 150 words. If it's a reviewer from a service, site, or a Top Reviewer, don't stumble through how you found them. They already know. Keep it succinct.

Don't give up. Those reviewers are almost as busy as literary agents. They aren't likely to respond to every request so keep at them if you really think they are a perfect fit for your book.

A Fiery Crash-Course in Facebook Ads for Indie Authors

I'll be the first to admit that I struggle with Facebook Advertisements. We have a love hate relationship—mainly because once I think I've found something that works for me, my hubris becomes my downfall. It is difficult to narrow down exactly what motivates consumers to make a purchase. I excel at this when face to face, but find using automated systems to grate my nerves. Alas, I cannot afford to spend 100% of my time on a sales floor, and so online advertising is a necessity.

Before you begin—make sure that you have all of the necessary pieces in place. Before wading into the choppy waters of Facebook Ads you should have already setup an author webpage, social media accounts (including an author one for Facebook which must be different than your personal account or Facebook won't give you access to ads,) an email service such as Mail Chimp or Constant Contact, and an optional blog.

Check your heart and head—are you purchasing ads to sell books and make money or are you trying to build up your audience? Understand that if you are trying to make bank by selling your books, Facebook ads probably shouldn't be your primary funnel. Effective ads are generally ones that help you break even and perhaps make a little profit. It has to be about more than the money—and if you are in charge of your own ads and promo as an author, then you're probably a relatively unknown commodity for now, so building brand awareness is worth the risk levied by adverts and reduced profit margins (everyone's got to pay the piper,) at this stage in the game.

Decide what you want to achieve—are you looking for more followers, email signups, drive website traffic, or are you trying to sell more copies of your book. I will concentrate on the latter for this article, although the principles are similar across the board. Also, for the sake of keeping it easy, we won't cover things like tracking conversions via pixel.

Do your research—just like you've got to be in the right audience to sell a fantasy novel or your nonfiction "choose your own adventure" knitting challenge to a live audience, you've got to know as much about the demographic you plan to advertise to as possible. Take advantage of the Audience Insight feature in Facebook's ad tools to get (scarily) detailed information on audience pools based on their likes and follows.

Cover appeal—as important as a book cover and rear cover text is to your physical novel, appealing graphics and ad copy are equally vital to the success of an advertisement. If you choose to run ads, don't do everything right up until now and then drop the ball here—that's like a fumble on the one-yard line. For graphics, make sure no more than 20% of your image is covered in text or the system will block it—be sure to set a hook with an amazing image that evokes emotion. For your ad copy, identify a pain to avoid or benefit to be gained by reading, use a call to action like "click to know more" or "sign up for mailing list," and try to create a sense of urgency.

Know your numbers—do the math with me. Remember when I said to check your heart? Let's check it against your wallet—by the time your book gets to the consumer, everyone will want to have gotten their cut. Let's look at a hypothetical 300-page 6x9 novel.

Reader pays $15 for book on Amazon. Amazon takes $6 for distribution and shipping. Createspace takes about $4.50 for printing. You now have about $4.50 in royalties—you can earn about another $0.25 if you set this sale up via an Amazon

Associates account, too. Facebook wants their advertisement money at the end when they charge you for everyone who clicked through your ad.

For the sake of the math let's assume a click costs you $0.20 and everything is typical about your budget and clickthrough averages for Indie book ads. The average clickthrough rate is 0.2% and the average conversion rate is 1-2% (that's one or two people buying your book for every hundred clicks). That's not good, but at least we know where the norm is. You need to get $4.50 in order to break even with one sale, but at two-tenths of a percent, you will have spent $20 for every $7.36 made at an average 1.5% conversion rate (*with Amazon Associates included*) meaning you lost almost $15 trying to sell your book. However, the low clickthrough rate means that for every book you sold, thousands and thousands of people had an ad on their screen, so at least there is some brand awareness being built at a deep level. But counting the cost is hard when it's this difficult to make the numbers match up to simply break even.

The solution is to reduce the cost per click… but that unbalances the metric and your ad will be shown much less often, so be aware of that.

Count the Cost—simply put, the conversion rate dictates your maximum spending if you insist on breaking even. To find that number, multiply your book's profit ($4.50) by the average conversion rate (1.5%) to get the number of cents you would want to cap your CPC at (6.75 cents). Markets fluctuate and change regularly, each month (even weekly) you should take the temperature of the advertisement to see how well it is selling (though you may have to guess, since traffic sent to Amazon for sales is difficult to separate from *all* sales). If your book is converting sales at something closer to ten percent your breakeven point is closer to $0.45. Constantly keep an eye on your numbers so you don't get hit with a giant bill and very little sales! Trust me. It's not fun.

The How-To: First, go to https://www.facebook.com/ads and click to create an ad. Select what you want your ad to do (send people to your link—your website, privately hosted page, or an amazon URL from your Associates account).

Follow the prompts in the wizard that will help you build your ad. Pick your demographic and input their likes, interests, etc. You want a very specific audience (use the Audience Insight feature to find them) that will be interested in your book and also likely to purchase. You want your target audience somewhere between 500,000 and 1,000,000 people; stay within those bookends or risk becoming unheard on the low-end or white noise on the high-end.

Set your placements, budget, and ad delivery details and save the info. The next part is to input your graphic, ad copy, URL, and anything else. The trick is to balance the ad so it is highly appealing, intensely targeted, and doesn't muddy the waters by overdoing it. It must be succinct and powerful.

Submit it when you are ready for it to go off to review by the Facebook Ad team for approval, and good luck. The turn-around is pretty quick. They want your money and sooner rather than later.

Many bloggers and experts advise steering clear of Facebook ads like they were a plague. Many have gone so far as to say that using Facebook ads to sell books is impossible to do without losing money. I see little results with them when I'm trying to push fiction, but do better than breaking even when I'm pushing my nonfiction, so there are some variables.

The jury is still out, and the market is constantly changing. Facebook ads are one tool in your marketing toolbox. I make the most sales when I'm selling person to person at events and make the most money when pushing Indie books that cost me less than five dollars to produce. Perhaps online marketing will get better, easier, and more profitable… perhaps you will find the key to success and never have to leave your writing cave, author hole, or coffee shop booth.

Give ads a try, but don't jump in headfirst… wade in slowly. This lake's got surprises for the unwary and the undertow is fierce.

10 Way-Points to an Online Sales Roadmap

I have a few tabs open on my phone's browser at all times--pages with some very basic advice I like to keep before me at all times. One of them has been Mike Fishbein's "How to Self-Publish a Bestseller." I've discovered that there is no such thing as a sure thing. You can follow this guide exactly and you are still not likely to "sell over 400 books in 10 days." This is one of those prime examples of articles written by the exception rather than the rule… However, it contains some very good, basic advice for indie authors and if you don't have a written strategy for how to get your book into peoples' hands other than airdropping them from your steam-powered dirigible at great personal expense (i.e. mass-giveaway due to your own independent wealth,) then this is a good structure to use as a starting point!

I would add a few points to his recommendations, but would start with this one: have a WRITTEN plan to fall back on. Just like I keep some tabs open until I've internalized every point, have something in print that you will see frequently as a reminder. It provides motivation to keep going—it will seem impossible, otherwise.

Q. How do you eat an elephant?

A. One bite at a time.

#1, Understand how Amazon's system works. It is a business and not a charity. If you want to succeed, know their metric for pitching sellable books to online shoppers and operate within the guidelines.

#2, Make sure your book is up to snuff. For the love of God, hire an editor, beg a beta reader, and be open to rewriting. Don't just "release a book into the wild." (Publish something on a whim and hope that lightning strikes).

#3, Have a good cover! We all judge books by their cover. Deal with it and understand that fact. Got it? Good, now go sell some blood to pay a cover designer for artwork. Freeware covers are okay for some genres (poetry, Christian devo, etc.) but are absolutely unforgiveable for others (fantasy, sci-fi, etc.)

#4, Have a good title. My nonfiction, Why Your Pastor Left, has hooked many people who intended to casually walk by a book signing table. Have you ever looked at a sign and not read it? No! our brains don't operate that way—take advantage of that automatic function. It's a sharp hook, make sure it's got a barb to keep your fish!

#5, Always be improving—this applies to your hooks/blurbs and descriptions at your online outlets. Feel free to go back and rewrite a product description if you think of a better wording.

#6, Get reviews! Beg if you have to. Without reviews, nobody will buy your book. Either live by this and keep trying or bury your head in the sand. There's no way around this one.

#7, Look at what others do for marketing. Mix it up with freebies, contests, etc. Don't balk at paid services for promotion—instead find something that will fit into your budget. (Expect to pay something, even if a low amount, in order to see success here.) Make a marketing plan that includes some kind of budget.

#8, Build your platform! Want people to see/discover you? You will have to be everywhere—and that risks eleventy-first Bilbo Baggins syndrome (becoming too little butter scraped across too much bread.) I made a written plan and schedule for social media posts, blogs, etc. I'm not where I want to be, but I keep plugging away at it. This won't happen overnight.

#9, Network with others. Don't look at other authors as competition... they will be your biggest supporters and sources of advice, comfort, and catharsis. Be someone who supports others—that means you may need to be proactive in reaching out. Need a place to start? Follow my blog or leave a comment on a post of mine, interact with me on social media. I'm making myself available to be your first follow/connection. Shoot me a message; even if not immediately I almost always find time to respond.

#10, Start somewhere—you won't be ready to sell 400 in ten days out of the gate, but maybe in a year after platform building you can achieve this. Take advice from others and keep working the system you've designed. You can do this... one blog at a time. One marketing attempt at a time. One tweet at a time. You don't have to start at point #1—the writing craft is a lot less linear than outsiders realize. Pick a reasonable place to begin and start working your plan—just make sure you start.

10 Important Things When Pitching Books at Conventions, Festivals, Trade Shows, etc.

This article is my most shared with fellow authors and available on my blog, too. Because many of us are far more comfortable behind the keyboard than behind the table at a book signing or in a convention booth, a lot of Indies need a little guidance in "how to sell."

I have some experience in sales. I did a lot of pitch-work for a national company and I ran my company's booth at all of our conventions back when I used to work in real estate, prior to that. I thought I'd share some things I've gleaned over time that have helped me sell books at these kinds of things.

Here are my top ten tips to running an author's booth at events.

1. Recognize that people didn't come to buy your book. You will have to sell them on it. Have ready a three-sentence elevator pitch, a longer version for those you've hooked, and a positive comparison to a well-known best seller, but with a twist. "My book is similar to Harry Potter, except that the main character is a girl with a speech impediment so she has trouble casting spells." (Yes, I just made that up–yes, I might actually write that story).

2. Do not sit down. This is basic sales 101. Nobody buys something from someone in a chair. There's a lot of psychology behind this. Feel free to disagree with me and sell fewer books, but if I'm talking to you at a convention about your book and you're so unenthusiastic about it that you can't stand (with physical disabilities being an obvious exception) then there's less than a 1% chance I'm going to take it home with me. Along with this, p*ut the book in their hand so they can feel a sense of ownership*

and possession on your book or item (it means they have to intentionally give it back and "say no" to buying it)–that's harder to do from a seated position.

3. Greet people and look them in the eye. Often this means people will stop and accidentally get sucked into a conversation which you can, and should, steer towards your book. (Look for openings to shift the conversation). It's fine if they walk away–often just drawing a crowd attracts other, more likely buyers. They see 1 or 2 others at your table and say "what's this interesting thing? I think I'll take a peek." Feel free to jump to the person with genuine interest and/or steer the conversation to include them in the sales pitch while the original party walked away. You can't sell to everyone, so try to determine which person is more likely to buy: it's usually person #2 in my experience.

4. Have a way to engage with people who walk away. A lot of people don't buy anything until they've seen it all and many might become interested but still have no intention of buying. Even knowing this, those people can still have some value: try to get them interested in joining a mailing list–I often run giveaways; each person who enters must give you enough info that you can add them to your mailing list after the event. If they're interested to read a *free* book, maybe they will eventually become interested enough to buy.

5. Make sure your family and friends understand that if they drop in on you at your table and an interested person comes to the table you're going to drop them like a hot brick… or a ton of potatoes… something like that. You are there for a purpose: to sell books. It's like having a job… no personal phone calls when you're on the clock. Yes, you're the boss, but small talk with family and friends are not the chief priorities when customers come. Customers usually won't wait for you, make sure your friends and

family know that… they've got to know they should take a step back and return to the conversation later.

6. Network with others. Arrive early and budget a little time to meet your neighbors and other, similar artists and authors also working the same event. They may or may not buy from you but that's not the goal. Networking is immensely valuable. You might have to opportunity to guest-blog, trade reviews, or work on other projects in the future that blow up into huge opportunities. Don't pass up that chance.

7. Don't leave! It should go without saying, but the less you are your table, the less likely you are to sell. It never fails, as soon as you step away people show up. Try to time your restroom trips and snack runs accordingly. If you can get something delivered or come prepared so you don't have to leave then all the better.

8. People don't ever come back! except when they do… but it's better to cut a deal and sell them something now than wait around expecting they will return and buy. From my sales training days in pitch-work I'd been told that something like 4% or less of those promising to return and buy a product actually do. Bird in the hand and all that… don't hold your breath on people coming back. Before they ever leave, ask them to put their info on your mailing list. (For some kinds of cons this return rate is much higher, so try to find out what your audience's buying temperature is and plan accordingly.)

9. Market yourself: make sure you have an appealing setup. Money spent on professional banners, postcards, and marketing materials that will catch the eye are worth it. Nobody will buy from you if they never see you. You're an introvert and don't want to engage people? Tough, role-play as an extrovert. Either fake it or hire someone to do it for you. You've got to grab attention in the three second window you've been given. At one con I attended my

booth-mate had his amazon sales page up so he could show interested people his reviews. That worked for him. There is no sure-fire set of materials to have so find what works–the only wrong choice is to forego them entirely.

10. Connect with readers. Ask everyone to leave a review in the usual places (Amazon, Goodreads, Smashwords, etc.) Spend extra time with those you are sure will read and review and seem to really engage with you. Remember that those readers you connect with are more likely to read through your entire back-list, buy your new titles, and recommend you to friends. Readers are awesome. Readers for life are better!

How Much Should Authors Charge for Speaking Engagements?

I rarely expect these sorts of requests, but the question came out of the blue, "How much do you charge to come and speak?" It may not happen to you early on as a writer, but you should have an idea in mind for a few reasons.

If you charge nothing (as you might think to as a knee-jerk reaction) people will assume you are worthless. I can attest to this personally from experiences across the arts. We used to run youth concerts all the time and attendance always suffered when the show was "free" because the inherent, subconscious value placed on the event was nothing. If there's no investment, there's no commitment and that means there's no value.

Your time is worth *something*. Even if you want to donate it or do a service for someone else or an organization there are travel fees (even if just fuel) which can sometimes be significant. You can do an event for free, but you should invoice the event with a figure to retain your "value." If you would normally charge $X.xx but do the event for free, ask for a gift in kind letter. If they are a nonprofit, like most libraries, they can supply you with that. You can write a reasonable speaking fee donation amount off on your taxes.

How much should you charge? It will vary widely depending on your area, but a good ballpark is about $200, from what I've heard from other authors (as a relatively unknown personality and hailing from a rural area). I ask for $200 from libraries and ask library workers to also identify one student reader who they think one of my books is perfect for but who might not be able to afford purchasing it—that student will receive a free, autographed copy.

If significant travel is involved I would ask for additional monies to cover expenses.

There are a few articles below that might help you to further think through things like speaking engagement fees, etc. In addition to being a writer I am a musician and regularly speak/preach at churches. As is often the case in religious work people tend to say, "oh, just pay me whatever you can afford/think it's worth." That's a pretty loaded position to put someone in. I booked a music and speaking gig and gave the church director a price. She was relieved to get it; over the past three years they'd used a different music team who incurred significant travel each year and she never knew if what they paid even covered expenses or was enough and so they always assumed they were imposing. Setting a fee and clearly stating what you will provide puts everyone at ease.

Have an idea what you want to charge. You don't need to be rigid, however. I tell libraries and organizations that I don't want cost to be an issue if it means the difference between doing an event or not and that we can negotiate something different if necessary.

Helpful links:
http://ask.metafilter.com/220256/How-much-should-I-charge-to-speak-at-an-event

http://author2author.blogspot.com/2012/06/what-should-i-charge-for-author-visit.html

https://writenaked.net/2014/02/24/qa-how-much-should-a-writer-charge-for-speaking-engagement/

Platform Building – Stay Engaged

When building a platform, we need to stay engaged with our readership. I mentioned before that people buy books from people—it's where Indie authors can really excel and find their footing—and it's something that Amazon and the big chains can never do as well as an Indie who is pounding the streets. A really good article came out over at the Marketing Christian Books Blog (one of the blogs I strongly suggest my audience follow—it's relevant to secular writers as well).

On the blog guest writer Dan Poynter asks point blank *"What am I willing to commit in time and energy each day or week to keep my book alive?"*

I think that it's important that authors don't like to themselves and realize that excitement and enthusiasm will wane during different periods—but that they should set some realistic goals (and if you're just starting and building a grandiose plan, your actual plan should probably be less than you think it is right now...just to keep it realistic and not burn out when it gets harder to find the committed time. Poynter also points out (as has my own contact at a publishing house,) that authors tend to put in a great effort to promote their book when it's been recently released but that effort slowly dwindles away until nothing remains.

He recommends something similar to my earlier article about platform building—a list of different possible actions to accomplish daily or weekly. Here is *his* list:

•Publish a new blog post or podcast at least once a week.
•Share your blog post on Reddit or StumbleUpon.
•Send a newsletter to your email list sharing your new blog post or podcast and reminding them of your book.

•Comment at least once a day on your social media accounts.
•Send a request to a book reviewer or blogger asking them to review your book.
•Join the discussion on online groups (Facebook, LinkedIn, Goodreads) that speak to your target audience or topic.
•Respond to a thread or start a new thread regularly.
•Write insightful comments on a blog that targets your audience or speak on your topic a couple times each week.
•Write articles and guest blog posts.
•Send a request to be a guest on a podcast that speaks to your topic or audience.
•Send thank you notes to people who share your social media posts, give you a shout out, air your blog post, interview you, or review your books.

I would offer a few caveats, however. There *is such a thing as going too far.*

• If you send an email every day your audience will stop reading. If you send one every week and the focus is on selling your book instead of recapping a blog or special thing you are doing beyond the book, people will unsubscribe because it's too sales-y.
•Don't be too overt in steering to your book—OR too dominant as an expert...be sure to it remains conversational; it's not a debate—it's a relationship.

Going Nuclear on Facebook Ads

If you are fortunate enough to get some good activity on your social media ads there are a few things you want to keep an eye on. I get a lot of traffic on the ad for my nonfiction book and thought I'd remind you that an advertisement has one purpose: to sell product.

My popular ad appropriately represents my book, <u>Why Your Pastor Left</u>, which addresses a very niche topic and helps people work through a difficult subject that is often fraught with pain and fresh struggle. It specifically targets certain keywords and an audience who has shown interest in major pastors, authors, and ministers—I know that the statistics of the problem mean that almost anyone with an active faith-walk who attends church will encounter this or has already. Not everybody is friendly to faith, however. If you've followed my blog or delve into its archives you will see that a certain segment of the population feels entitled to troll faith-writers and villainize people who believe differently—I'll come out and say it: it's usually atheists who can't handle opposing viewpoints or logic that doesn't coincide with their emotions.

That probably sounded like a digression… but it's not. Whatever side of the aisle you sit on or whether you attend a church, mosque, or none at all you will discover that most of the world is very small-minded and violently reactive. You can post a photo to social media of yourself with a giant tomato you grew in your garden and find snarky comments in short order from people asking if you're secretly working with Monsanto or have injected GMOs into the fruit (as if that's how it works). Most people don't really know what a GMO is, but that doesn't stop them from vomiting on your happiness. It's what humans do—and we do it well… we do it frequently because we think that sitting on this side of the keyboard somehow protects us and makes our ideas bigger and better than they are. For some reason, we think the internet is anonymous and provides carte blanche to be a jerk.

Back to my ad—something you need to do is keep a handle on responses and comments. It is nice to have a high comment count. My ad had about hundreds comments the first time I ran it crawled high again the second time around as people asked questions and left thoughts on the topic. Most of them haven't even read the book. Those belligerent social justice warriors I mentioned above? I've deleted dozens of comments such as "your pastor left because he was probably caught diddling children" and "he left because he realized god is a figment of stupid people's imagination."

When you run an ad for your book remember that the ad is not a public forum! You do not have to leave nasty comments up. You should not negotiate with trolls or justify inflammatory comments with a response. You are in complete control and you can AND SHOULD exercise nuclear authority. Delete and ban antagonists. Your ad's goal is to sell product, anything that doesn't somehow contribute to that goal should be removed.

Trolls flock to anything that generates an audience for them to fling poo at. It's what trolls do, so don't let their opinions bother you. Advertisements are meant to help *you* and are paid for by *you*—so don't let anyone hijack your promo vehicle.

Signing Books at Chain Stores

For a long time, I did not do much by the way of book signings... primarily because of a lack of success in my early history with it. Most of those early stores were smaller, mom and pop shops in non-metropolitan communities. I wanted to change that and so I contacted the Barnes & Nobles near an event I was already booked at in the hopes that I could possibly double up on my promo to maximize my travel dollars. No dice... but mainly because of other bookings and a temporary snafu with my publisher's listing within Ingram that didn't have my title listed as returnable at that time.

After some pleasant conversation and asking for a referral from one manager at a store I used to frequent in my college days I finally got the right person on the phone (that's always key) – you want to talk to their Community Business Development Manager, or CRM. I set up a date and time to call her in a month to revisit the conversation after I'd verified with my publisher that the changes were setup within Ingram's catalogue before calling her back. We set a date for a few months down the road and I did some cross-promotion for the event at local cons and outlets

I knew I wanted to learn as much as I could to help me secure more bookings for the future. I picked the brains of two store managers and asked for honest feedback on what I did during my two-hour timeslot in the store. My articles about pitching to buyers and browsers during conventions, festivals, and fairs turned out to be relevant. "Basically, everything you did was perfect and the prime example of what we want to see authors do," the manager told me as I wrapped up my roller bag with promo tools inside. "Too many authors come in and sit at the table expecting people to stop, but they don't. You engaged our customers and that was the number one thing."

As I mulled over my thoughts, I was glad that I didn't appear too ostentatious. My voice travels, especially when I'm adding enthusiasm or excitement to my voice—which I always do when pitching my books. Deep down I was scared that they might prefer authors to remain hands off, but realized after his feedback that *they* bought a bulk order of my books and now own them. *They* want my help selling them so that *they* can make a profit (literally, they get more money per book then I do as the author—that's how it works sometimes.) It makes sense that they want a free salesman to help move the units. I thought over the whole experience on my long drive home and compiled a list of Ten Things to keep in mind when doing a Barnes and Nobles or chain-store book signings:

•DO NOT use your chair. I didn't sit down once during the signing. I've said this a bunch of times before. "Nobody buys books from you if you're sitting unless it's in a wheelchair." The manager agreed.

•Everybody eavesdrops. Be excited and boisterous when you explain your book to someone. It may pull in other potential buyers (even if your first customer wanders away.) About a third of my sales were to people who came over because they overheard me describing a book to someone else and it intrigued them.

•Be Visual/Be Seen. The manager appreciated the fact that I had professional, quality banners and signage that helped point out the event to customers (remember, THEY WANT YOU TO SELL A TON OF BOOKS!) Marketing materials are worth their weight in gold—and the best part is that many are reusable. Invest wisely in this area.

•Ask for feedback. Not only does it keep you humble and teachable but it strokes the ego of a manager. Helping make his or her day better is never a bad idea. Remember that you are there *to help them* sell books, not bolster your own self-worth. It's a valid trade: you provide them with a little slave labor and receive some platform building/marketing clout in exchange. During your signing, mentally remind yourself that you work for them—so ask them how you can best meet their needs.

•Don't make assumptions about the store or the staff. It should go without saying, but remember, the lesson above. It's okay to ask for specific boundaries so you don't accidentally break a local policy, etc.

•Don't MAKE DEMANDS. The manager told me how many authors ask for a different location because they think it will put them in contact with more people/better visibility. Understand that they probably put you somewhere specific for a reason and are likely more familiar with what makes a successful event in their store than you are. Be grateful. They didn't have to let you come and don't have to let you return. You can ask for something else or make a suggestion—just don't go bridezilla on them or you'll get left at the altar.

•Start random conversations! I often look for ways to engage someone. I saw an eleven-year-old in a Marvel Heroes shirt walking nearby and asked him who his favorite hero was. We bonded, he looked at my books and became my biggest fan. His dad bought two of my four books. Sometimes I even catcall to people who try not to look at me because they don't want to engage in conversation, are in a rush, etc. I'll say "Hey!" and then something weird (but not inappropriate) and say in an awkward voice "Oh no! I was trying not to get suckered into a conversation with that guy by avoiding eye contact and now I'm stuck—somebody help me!" If you make someone laugh, sometimes they come back. Sometimes they even buy books—just don't be rude about it. Engage someone like a friend, not a crusty circus carnie. The key word is *engage*, not *alienate*.

•DO MAKE ASSUMPTIONS ABOUT CUSTOMERS (but don't ever, ever, ever tell them that.) When someone is carrying a similar genre title in the store it gives you a hint about their preferences (It's not always right—it could be a gift—but hedge your bet it's for them). The same goes for dress and appearance. People usually have a type. We're all walking billboards for our personal preferences—we just need to learn how to read them. Are they wearing a Final Fantasy T-shirt or have a Pikachu tattoo on their neck or sport an Ash Ketchum hat? Your historical fiction book may not be the best fit and if he is about to walk by at the same time as an older woman with bifocals who is carrying Killing Lincoln, I know which person I'm going to try to engage. If you turn out to be wrong in your guesses, it's usually easy enough to backtrack and take a new angle.

•Connect with people. People are only half-buying your book because they think it will be good. The other 50% is because they were sold on *you*. They are literally paying for this hunk of ink and paper because they met you and felt that an interaction with the author was worth an added value. Don't discount the relationship opportunities! It's why you're in the store so make every effort to connect with people. Give them reasons to become fans instead of just customers.

•Believe in yourself. Don't be timid. The store CRM probably vetted you and your book at least to some degree… they went as far as to purchase some books, so they've invested in this thing because *they believe in you*. All those people coming through the doors? most of them came with money and the intent to buy a good read. Is your book good? Then sell it! It's got to be good or you wouldn't be at the store trying to pimp your story for nickels and 5-star reviews. If you're afraid it's sub-par then it was never ready for release and you need to pull it from the shelves, go back to editing, and not send it back into the wild until it's got teeth. You must believe this book is a story that these people need to read. It's your story. It's the best story. They came to buy one—so make sure you don't deprive them of the greatest thing they're going to read this year.

A few bonus ideas for the uninitiated.

• Have the customer purchase the book before you sign it. I learned the hard way that sometimes people will bail at the register or will have forgotten their wallet and then you have a personalized piece of merchandise that will never sell.
•Whatever you do, own it… just don't be cocky. You're probably doing these events because you're not making six digits off your writing right now. If you did make a killing last year, feel free to disregard everything here and do your own thing. That's cool… and email me what you're doing so I can learn.
•Always ask a customer to spell their name. It's pretty awkward when the "Jeff" you just autographed with a Sharpie tells you, "Actually it's Geoff." True story—learn from me.
•Send a thank you to follow up.

At the end of my slot the manager told me I was welcome back any time. I also asked him for any outlets, stores, or people I ought to contact next. Don't underestimate name-dropping or honest advice. I hope this article helps you!

Using Amazon Associates

At first, I nearly gave up on the Associates program, having used it a loooong time ago (back before everyone was even on Amazon.) It's changed much since then. Given the potential benefits possible to use the program in conjunction with social media ads I decided to flounder my way through the Amazon Associates program and relearn it—I got kicked out of the program multiple times. Their rules are very draconian and they will shut you down over simple things, so fair warning: it may take a little bit to get everything just right. While their customer service is quick to respond, they can't undo your account's cancellation and you will have to start again from scratch with the slightest error.

After much time online with customer service I realized two things. 1. How to fix the hiccups and 2. Indies *really need* to take advantage of this program. I'll break down both points.

As mentioned, I got kicked out of the program multiple times. The first one is no big deal—it was an old account I had opened with them back when the program first started in the early 00s when I did occasional reviews on my early website (I'm talking 15+ years ago.) Obviously, it lapsed into inactivity over a decade ago and I'd never made any money off it—plus the account terms and conditions had changed since then. It really has no bearing on the topic accept to point out that it caused some confusion since all the old account info in their system never goes away; Amazon archives them for tax purposes—even closed accounts. Watch out for that in case you've got an old account with them and make sure you're logged into the right account—thinking you're in the right account will cause lots of problems if you didn't check, first.

At first, I set up an Astore via Associates so that I could sell my books on my website with its online cart-based system. People tend to follow other links, however, and so they made purchases through Amazon directly. Three months later my Associates account is killed by Amazon citing inactivity—if you don't make a sale they shut you down. The account cannot be reinstated. I was a little miffed that there was no warning, but I did know that there was a 3-month period going into it. A warning really would've been nice—I mean, Amazon is a pretty big outfit, you'd think their fancy algorithms could find some time to say, "Dear Human, in a few days we will close your account unless you feed me those delicious internet hits." Side note, they no longer offer the Astore feature and it's really not the best use of the program, anyway… it's not how people shop anymore.

Second verse, same as the first. I made a new account, this time I put more attention and effort into it and was a little excited because Christmas was coming. My book sales had been increasing and I realized that I'd really been using the program wrong. I use Facebook ads and had never set my links as affiliate ones (links I'd make money off of,) in the ads. I went through and changed all my advert links after building them through my affiliate account. I was excited and wanted to check them and see the affiliate tracking program at work and so I used my own affiliate links to purchase a few books as Christmas gifts.

WORD TO THE WISE: *Don't do that*. I was basically just testing it out, but those fancy Skynet Algorithms flagged me for account violations. *Spending your own money* on a product from an ad that *you paid to place* on their behalf is an egregious violation. (Truthfully, I understand why they don't want you to do that, but it an immediate account cancellation!)

Amazon is very Third-Reich about participation in their programs… I suppose is self-preservation. I'm sure some hackers or moneygrubbing cybermen setup bots to take advantage of the system and the rest of us humans have to live under iron clad rules.

Another word of warning, when you set up your account, you will want to list your website and blog but not your Facebook or twitter. If you do not have tens of thousands of followers (Amazon is vague to the actual number they want) they will schedule it for deletion. You get the picture. The program is run by Daleks yelling "Delete! Delete!"

DON'T LIST ANY SOCIAL MEDIA ACCOUNT ON YOUR AMAZON PROFILE UNLESS YOU'RE A CELEBRITY.

Finally, I came at it one last time but did it slower—rather than changing all my ad links and everything right away (every time I got deleted I lost several hours' worth of work,) I got back into the program and changed just one link. I compared my work to some of what others were doing and searched for specific problems others had encountered. When I didn't get booted out I finally moved forward.

I found a nice article here that helped: https://marketever.com/mistakes-get-banned-amazon-affiliate/

Sales started coming in and my account was approved. I probably won't make a cool trill... or even a million... but sellers can certainly make some real cash from their system—you're not going to make more money than Amazon, but the Associates program *is a way to get even more money off every book you sell* when you promote your book as an Indie author.

Despite the learning curve, if you're an Indie author you really ought to be using this program.

Using Amazon Associates is kind of like filing taxes when you're poor. If you don't file, you are leaving money on the table by not claiming refunds and credits available to you. If you don't file you are essentially "leaving money on the table." Yes, it's a little work to get it, but it can really pay off.

Here's a breakdown on the dollars and cents for a hypothetical book. Let's say we can sell about 50 copies in a month: 20 paperbacks, 20 Kindle, and 10 audible, making 4.50, 3.50, and 3.00 each, respectively—you may be way lower or higher, but it's a good starting place for many indie authors. For the sake of the argument let's say that each sale came from a FB ad you purchased and every sale went through your affiliate link. The total is $190 profit. Let's say it takes about 800 hits on a FB ad to make those 50 sales but you're paying .09 per click on average (see my other blogs about setting up ads). That was $72 spent on ads (you made $118! Yay!) An affiliate account pays you an advertisers commission on *anything* you sell: at this number, it would be about 6.5% off net, which in our hypothetical book's case, is about $500 giving you an additional $32.50 which really helps offset that ad budget—it's money left on the table that Amazon will just keep if they don't pay that commission.

The commission is already built in to Amazon's pay structure. Our hypothetical book in the above scenario is retailing at $15 and costs about $4 purchase as an author copy via Createspace. You're making $4.50 and it costs about $4 to make, so what about the other $5.50? That's the profit margin which goes to Amazon and all their programs (free shipping, distribution, etc.) They've built into it at least an extra buck and half to pay for that commission setup which is run on a sliding scale based on how much you sell (Amazon Associates cap the ratio at 8.5% provided you sell and ship 3,131 items or more per month.)

I know that I hate spending money with no or little return and it always makes it difficult for me to venture my hard-earned money to pay for internet ads. Here's something to help you breathe easier. Let's say someone clicks our ad for a hypothetical book and isn't really into it but sees on the product listing, "Customers who viewed this item also viewed…" and they decide instead to purchase *Fifty Shades of Gandalf the Grey* for $25 (A high price because I assume that book would really necessitate being read in *hard*cover.)

Your Associate's account will record a $25 sale and you will get commission on it once it's paid for and ships. Let's say our hypothetical customer (Sally is an aging Kindergarten teacher with a vanilla marriage and a sketchy past—she secretly moonlights as a bounty hunter for bond-skippers,) doesn't check out just yet. She leaves the browser open and decides her husband (his name is Jack and he's got his own history as a high-stakes Magic the Gathering player who really needs to win the pot at a back-room game at Wizardcon or he'll lose the house!) could really use a Black Lotus proxy card. He adds it to the cart for another $15 purchase towards your sales totals. (I know, you can't buy proxies on Amazon, but I didn't want the scenario to be *too* realistic.)

The nice thing about the Associate link tag is that you get credit for *all of the purchases made within that browsing session.* A customer you sent to Amazon might not buy your book, but you can still earn sales and get a percentage off of those purchased items!

It may be new territory for you as a writer, but Indie authors have to be their own sales staff, promo team, and wear a million other hats as well. Take some time to learn the system and work it to your advantage. It's in your best interest.

It may feel like you're betraying your call as a writer to spend a bunch of time on other non-writing aspects of being an Indie author, but as Chuck Sambuchino says in his writing conferences, "It's called getting paid." Sometimes we do what we must in order to do what we want, and this is something you can add to an existing promotion structure to make it pay off just a little more.

Don't leave your money on the table. If you do, someone else is bound to claim it.

How NOT to Promote Your Book

I see many Indie authors promote stuff on pages for authors. Good job. You did it. Handclap emoji. You wrote a book... yay. That's cool. But I'm probably not going to buy your book. Most author groups I'm a part of exist to give support and feedback to fellow writers. Most of those promo posts are downright "salesy."

Promotion is necessary, but most Indies do it wrong. Pitching your book exclusively in author circles is probably gonna leave you with a low glass ceiling for sales numbers. Lots of support and love... muchas reviews, yes. Cash money? Probably not so much. Remember, those authors are all looking for their own sales and promotions avenues, too.

If you join XYZ Author's Facebook Group your goal should be to network, NOT to promote. Promotion is white noise, there. Inevitably the people I see post most often in those places post lots of messages. 1. Greetings, I'm the author of ABC Book, please check it out here. 2. I'm so proud that ABC Book got reviewed by so and so. Please read my book. 3. Here's an ad for ABC Book. 4. I'm doing a book signing and you should all come, here are the details. 5. I'm doing a special sale on ABC Book—here's the link. Lather. Rinse. Repeat.

Personally, I have a promo plan I follow every week in order to grow my platform and network with others--this isn't sales exclusive. I know I've lost that focus in the past and that lack of realistic expectations can make me feel like I'm spinning my wheels in the mud.

I'll be blunt. If you only post in social, authors' groups and expect you've met some kind of social media marketing mandate in doing so, you will only sell a limited number of copies and your networking will fall flat. Networking groups want to get to know *you* first, and then learn about your book. With constant pitching, you'll maybe sell a couple books, sure, but those numbers are a false positive and you'll eventually hit a wall and not know why because "it worked before... why aren't I selling any groups in *The Stay-at-Home Mom Fellow Authors Group* anymore?"

These groups are a bit like real life relationships. If you've been invited to a regular coffee gathering and every time you speak you bring up Amway, ItWorks, or any kind of multi-level-marketing thing you're involved in, the group might just change their meeting time/location and never tell you about it. I know they say, "always be selling," but that isn't always appropriate. Sometimes, in some places, you have to sell yours*elf* first in order to keep that door open. It's called human interaction or building relationships.

Groups like this are one foot of a multi legged stool. I'm just cautioning against it being someone's *only* avenue (or only posting when trying to sell--that's a good way to become a tiresome nuisance to those who use the group to interact and network.) There are some groups exclusively used for selling--it's a whole different mindset and both have a different purpose. One is for authors, the other is for stories. Remember which is which and use them properly or you risk getting yourself blacklisted from online author communities and/or blocked on social media.

How to Create Coupon/Discount Codes for Createspace Paperback Books

I wanted to offer discounts as an added bonus to friends and readers who subscribed to my mailing list (BTW, you should totally signup here for that... opt in to my OFFICIAL MAILING LIST and see firsthand how the system works. You can find it on my website authorchristopherdschmitz.com).

Right at the get-go I want to mention that this method does not give you coupons for Amazon.com. It only gives you coupons for the Createspace eStore. Yes, they are all the same, but there is a difference on the customer's experience. It's a different sales portal than Amazon.

You make more money per sale if a book is purchased directly via Createspace—while Amazon owns Createspace, they have different front-end and back-end systems. That said, Amazon is a middle-man reseller and takes their cut for housing your book on their digital shelves, just like any brick-and-mortar store would. I would suggest creating your own e-book store on your personal author website (don't have one? Get one! Like, before you finish reading this sentence. You need one.) Some services will allow you to use your own point of sale system and integrate the CS bookstore into it.

The up-side to Createspace is more money and the ability to grant coupons (even down to the point where you make nothing on a sale if you wish.) The down-side is that it's not directly through Amazon's interface (which shoulders the burden of consumer confidence) and there aren't options for free shipping. The Createspace store interface is clunky and inconvenient—and this is intentional. Consumers prefer the Amazon shopping experience and the company knows that… however they are unwilling to change the storefront because that would make it compete with itself and means Amazon would lose money from its position as the middleman. Indies have been complaining about this for years but Amazon is simply not interested in making less money per sale (go figure.) That's just the nature of the business.

For the purposes of this post, I will use my Sci-fi novel Dekker's Dozen: The Last Watchmen. You can see the Createspace store page by looking at it here: https://www.createspace.com/6178667 (BTW, if you want to buy it, you can a 10% discount with this coupon code we will build to demonstrate this article. Use coupon code: GK4AEER4)

Step One:

Where the heck is your Createspace book link? It's hiding in the circled, tiny link.

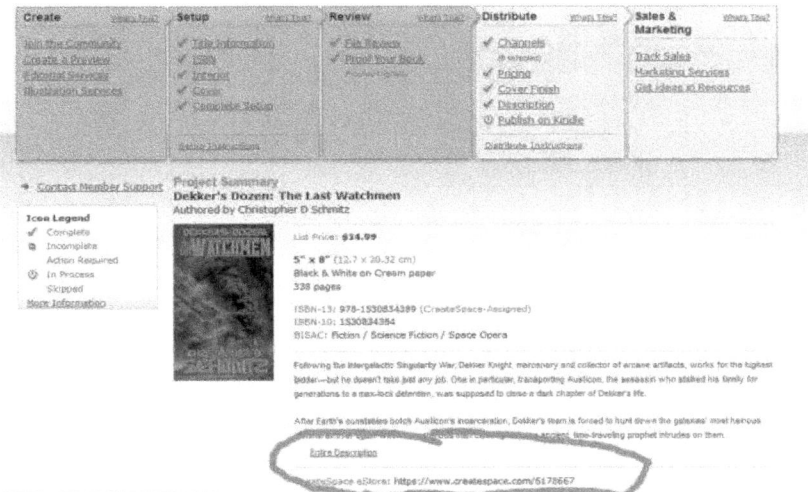

Step Two:

Go to your Sales Channels page. Make sure that the Createspace eStore is selected as a possible sales channel (it is selected by default). You have limited control to setup how your page looks under the Setup link and you can create coupons under the Discount Codes link. The system is a little clunky. You have to go through a separate setup page to get a code and then go back to enter the code and its discount amount—also, you don't get to pick what the codes are, but it is a functional system… not as crisp as the method for doing eBook coupons via Smashwords, but this is the best method to giving coupons for paperback copies.

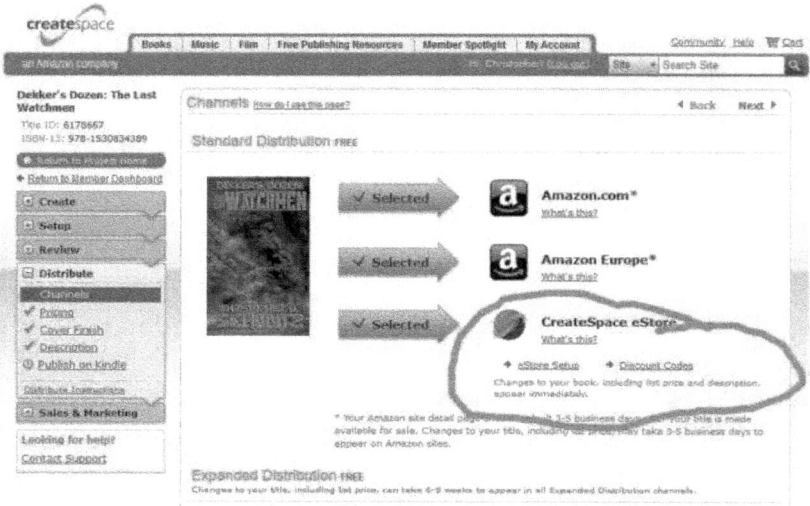

How to Create Coupon Codes for Smashwords eBooks

While Smashwords eBooks might be slightly more difficult to actually put together so that they pass all of the quality control checks (a system in place because the file has to meet minimum requirements for *all* of the formats out there, not just those of Kindle or iTunes,) the coupon system is more user friendly than that of Createspace.

I'll show you how to set up a coupon for a graphic novel I commissioned as a promo tool. The electronic version of the comic was always meant to be a free giveaway for any readers who sign up for my author's mailing list. I have my Mail Chimp autoresponder set to give readers who opt-in a link with the discount code we will make. When someone enters the discount code in the coupon box it will change the price to zero during checkout.

Log into your Smashwords dashboard and find the title you want to make a coupon for. Find and click the Coupon button as pictured.

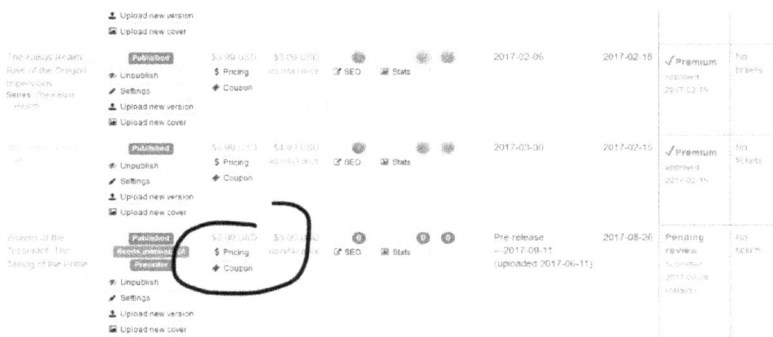

On the following page, the Coupon Code Manager you will see all the coupons that exist for that title. Since it is empty, click Generate Coupon to get this page.

Generate Coupon Code for Wolves of the Tesseract: The Taking of the Prime

Regular price:	$4.00
Coupon discount:	100 % off (1 to 75, or 100)
New promotional price:	$ 0.00 (0.99 to 3.99, or 0.00)
Projected proceeds from each sale:	$ 0.00
Coupon expires:	August ⌄ 1 2022 Please choose a date that is after tomorrow and not farther than 5 years. Expirations are on a California calendar of GMT -08:00.
Description, (for your personal reference)	Mailing List Giveaway
Metered redemptions: (leave blank for unlimited, otherwise enter number to limit number of redemptions)	
Make this a public coupon:	☐ A private coupon code is visible only to people you share it with. A public coupon code is visible to all visitors of your Smashwords book page, and the special discount price appears most other places around the site where your book gets listed, while browsing book categories, in search results, on your profile page, etc. Books with public coupons also appear in the "Special Deals" section of the Smashwords site. Public coupon codes are seen by more readers; otherwise, the two codes work the same. You can go back and change this setting at any time.

Generate Coupon

As you can see, there are more tools and more powerful options available to you through the Smashwords system including the ability to meter redemptions, set expiration dates, and include the listing in a special deals section if you make the coupon publicly available. Since my purposes are promotional, I created a second coupon deal for the book and made that one public.

This is a great way to give your subscribers something free or to share your book with reviewers or blogs without the need to attach files to emails or worry about sending incompatible format versions for your reader's devices.

Experiment with Smashwords. They put a lot of powerful tools at your disposal provided you can divert traffic to them rather than Amazon (though Smashwords also pushes distribution to Amazons competitors such as B&N, iTunes, etc. for digital books.)

Best practice for Giving Away Free Books

One of the most widely used tools for Indie authors is the book giveaway. It can inspire a quick following and even generate real sales if used correctly. It is not, however, as easy as setting your price to free, sitting back, and watching your download counter tick skyward like a fuel pump.

A book giveaway is not by any means a magic bullet that turns into a massive, new readership. However, if you follow a few simple steps you can maximize your results and it might spark up interest in your book—particularly if you have a back list (other books that curious shoppers will find by clicking through your author profile.)

First, understand that a giveaway is a means to promote and advertise. There are companies that specialize in doing this for profit. What I mean by this is: it's something that many people invest time and money into… you won't succeed if you only give it paltry efforts. Planning is important.

Persuading shoppers to buy a book typically moves people through a process called "The Funnel." The funnel is a channel that moves people from discovery to fandom; it's sometimes been called AIDA by seminar hosts. The four basic steps are

Attention

Interest

Desire

Action

Attention. A reader learns about you though some means of awareness (a promo, advert, recommendation, or seeing the book on a shelf.)

Interest. Something must kindle their curiosity and draw him or her to the title.

Desire. Provided their expectations are met after reviewing the contents or blurb, they want to take it home. This hopefully means a move to…

Action which results in a purchase. It might also present itself as signing up for a mailing list, shelving a book on Goodreads, or bagging it in a wish-list.

Understanding that structure begs the question of strategy. How will you get attention? Will your ad copy, cover, and content generate interest and desire? What is the Action you want purchase, platform following, or awareness? (If you don't know that, you ought to figure it out first. Don't just give away a book because some blog said it would be helpful—that's how you lose money and gain frustration.) Typical Action items Indies want are Likes/Follows on social media, signing up for mailing lists, increased shares/attention, and continued promo/visibility (added to lists in Goodreads, etc.), book purchases from backlists or associated titles, and reviews. Your intended Action step/outcome helps to determine the other components.

Also, remember that you can giveaway other items than your book—that's important to keep in mind when crafting the Action step. Many people giveaway gift cards, items such as a free Kindle or eBook reader, etc. Just keep in mind that Amazon's search and destroy algorithms sometimes take issue with reviews posted by people who received a gift card from an author they later reviewed (resulting in said review being deleted).

Ask yourself how you will bring attention to the giveaway. Many readers go in search of them through Amazon's kindle freebie lists and many do the same for Goodreads' paperback giveaways. Larger networks such as these (and others like LibraryThing) have a built-in network which someone else has worked hard to craft, like Bookbub's famous mailing list. Those places may or may not charge a fee for you to access their platform. You will need to decide if that will be a worthwhile endeavor for your publicity. There are many free and paid options available. In my experience, the expensive ones are often worth it and see a return (the same for most free places since there's no cost except for time), while the cheapest paid services have consistently been a waste of money for me. Don't buy generic advertising unless you've got a solid referral from someone who used it.

When setting up a giveaway don't forget the timeliness of it. Use a calendar with alerts. You will want to increase your social media presence and use every promotional tool in your arsenal. Run the contest for long enough that readers can find you and sign up, however, don't run the promo for too long or readers' interest will peter out. Give away more than a single copy to increase interest. You should be prompt with your fulfillment, too, but exercise wisdom and check out contest winners. One of my Goodreads giveaway resulted in a winner for an overtly religious book I had written. Her profile claimed that her favorite fiction genre was F/F Slash (which, if you don't know, is lesbian fanfiction erotica.) I felt pretty certain that she would not like my book and explained why while offering a different book I had published that she might find better suited to her tastes. She took me up on the offer. While I did not get a review out of it, I almost certainly avoided a negative one.

There are many services that will help you run your giveaway and collect/generate data on your behalf. Check out Rafflecopter, KingSumo, and ShortStack.

Experts recommend focusing attention on one or two things at a time to maximize success.

I hope this helps you as a guide to crafting your own publicity events with free giveaways.

Be a Rockstar at Book Signings

I often schedule book signings at chain bookstores. They are somewhat intimidating at first. If you work it properly and do the right due diligence beforehand you will be just fine. I usually do well enough at them, but something didn't quite seem right at one as I got everything together. I realized what it was: this store treated authors like music venues tend to treat musicians. You might be thinking "I'd love to be a rockstar!" But that's not what I mean. Most modern venues have a habit of abusing artists and don't hide the attempt to steal their platforms, or at the very least, profit greatly from it. It's often called *Pay to Play* by bands not working the national scene and I'll explain how it's bad for authors and bad for music artists.

For most venues since the rise of social media, the thought has gone like this:

1. Artist has friends/followers. 2. Require overtly or implicitly that their friends must show up. 3. Capitalize on the built-in fan-base. 4. Require all promotion, advertising, etc. be done and paid for by artist; the venue might hang a flyer. 5. Collect money from fan-base for purchases (and possibly even require bands to pay cash in order to perform.)

Some are overt, other payments come as hidden fees for "equipment/stage rental," sound-guy fee, etc. It actually gives me a SpongeBob SquarePants flashback from the episode where SpongeBob gets the fry cook job and negotiates an initial salary of paying Mr. Krabs only $100 an hour to labor for him.

Many bookstores have caught onto this model. While generating less sales, it requires zero investment and no work on the part of the staff (and usually the person booking an author event is the same person who would have to do this extra legwork). This has typically been the norm in smaller, Indie stores; it seems like relations managers at bigger chains have keyed in on this too, now.

Here's the story in a nutshell. The store (in a medium-sized town about two hours from my home) was eager to discuss a signing. The venue continually asked me how much I was planning to spend on adverts and how many of my local friends I could expect to come and buy books in the store along with whatever other shopping they might do, (just like paying a cover charge and then buying drinks at the venue). Firstly, *those are reasonable questions to ask.* A store would want that info in order to adequately prepare.

After explaining how well I'd done in one of the chain's sister stores, I told them how many books I'd expect to sell (15-20) in my time there with a similar setup and gave them estimates on how many books they should buy. They completely ignored all the data I gave them.

I got there and they didn't have me setup anywhere visible to the customers, in fact, I was barely able to see or talk to a customer until after the shoppers had already checked out and headed back for the exit. (I should've probably asked to be moved—I did arrive early, so that's on me, but I had assumed they would want to put me in the best place for success. That just wasn't so.)

I learned a lesson and I'm now explicit on what I'd like my setup to look like and where I'd like to be placed. The store also ordered more than twice what I'd recommended they buy. I really tried to sell ten books—but didn't quite make even that given the set up. The store sent *all the books back the next day,* even though some of my local contacts did go to the store mid-week looking for them. Because they'd ordered so many I had to pay return shipping to Ingram. I actually lost money for every book they carried because of the slim profit margin on larger books plus the return shipping costs for fifty books. It was a pretty bad weekend if I was only going to make money (add in costs of travel, food, etc.) luckily networking is the primary reason I do these.

Once the event wrapped up, I had that distinctly dirty feeling that I got whenever my band had a poorly attended concert because a venue had done nothing but prey on our platform.

Before I sound like a cranky old miser, I should probably note that managers don't necessarily intend to trip you up—they just want to do less work or perhaps they don't realize how they are turning potentially successful events into difficult ones. Education and clear communication helps fix that.

There has to be a happy medium where stores partner with readers. Sometimes fans will come in to see an author (I often generate a handful, but those people usually have my books already,) but an author is really there to help the store make more sales and connect with readers on a more meaningful level.

Of the customers I was able to talk with at this signing-gone-wrong, I sold more books by other people than my own; I always make book recommendations or help direct shoppers to other parts of the store. Even with unmet expectations you can still uphold your part of the commitment.

To ensure better success, have a specific checklist of requests for the store and be upfront about how you are there to help them sell books. You will be more successful if they:

•Put you where you can make eye contact with people as they enter the store. Proximity is important.
•Make announcements every 30-60 minutes via intercom
•Take out social medias ad and/or tag local readers they think

might enjoy your book based on genre
•Have the signing area prepped and ready prior to my arrival. •Set a copy of my books at the register with a sign stating the signing/autograph details and times—if they could do this a few days in advance that's a bonus! Also handy is a sign that you're willing to autograph pre-purchased books at the event and leave them with the manager to be picked up later for those who can't attend.
•Shelving your book in the proper genre section a week prior is helpful—as is a partial endcap display announcing the event.
•Use wisdom and have reasonable expectations for book sales

Here's the moral of the story: don't do book events to make money. Be happy to break even. Find the most economic ways to get to the signing, keep your costs down, and go with the attitude that you're there to meet, greet, and network in order to build up future success. Understand that the stores don't really care that much about you—they are in the business of selling books. Help them do that, but also help them understand that you can't help meet their needs if they have set you up to do otherwise.

Since becoming clearer with my requests for how a store prepares for my event I've sold more books and had better events. Know what you want and how you and a store can work together best. Be smart, and happy selling.

Books-A-Million Hates Indie Authors

Despite the inflammatory title, they may or may not actually hate us. I'm picking on them because they are the biggest chain store with rules that specifically shut out Indies. Other stores have similar rules, and so do certain catalogue book services such as CBD (Christian Book Distributors

I had a Books A Million store want to do an author signing in their store. I have a few fans in Iowa where the only bookstore in town was a BAM and I was traveling through in a few months for a publishing expo in Chicago so I'd hoped to do something on the way. The manager shot me up his chain of command to try and get it set up.

After jumping through hoops with their extremely reluctant-to-talk corporate guys via email I was told they would not authorize it and that there is no wiggle room in their rules. They have dedicated book buyers who purchase bulk titles from major publishers, those books go to a BAM warehouse and sit until stores request them. It's the old-school way of the book business and only allows for books with print runs of thousands of copies. No Print on Demand allowed.

It doesn't matter that I have a following in an area near their store, not does it matter that the manager was excited and wanted me to come. Under no circumstances will BAM carry a book that was printed at a POD press/distributor—even if that press is a smaller/mid-sized traditional publisher. If it hasn't sat on a shelf in a warehouse somewhere, they refuse to let it in their stores. Of course, they still want you to sell it through their online portal where they can enjoy the convenience of making profit without the overhead of storage (the main point of POD, making their position pure hypocrisy.)

Their iron-clad dictum is a huge slap in the face of Indie writers across the board. It shows the companies unwavering allegiance to the giant book machine that churns out only mass-produced rewrites of the last "big thing" that corporate suits decided was good literature—a setup that guards against new voices in the industry. It stifles creativity and force-feeds readers the same old stuff. Not that all of it is bad (I enjoy Crichton and King, but wouldn't have read many great stories had I not also pulled titles from the Indie market). Really, there is much truth in Pierre Tristam's column when he responded to a New York Times Article about bookstores, BAM in particular. (see https://flaglerlive.com/65608/end-of-bookstores-pt)

Tristam predicts that big chains will eventually go out of business because of their self-serving interests. "They're to literature what Steak and Shake is to good food. They have merchandise, but they have no soul… When's the last time our Books-A-Million hosted a writer's reading, an interesting lecture, a book party of any sort? The company is too interested in pushing marketing gimmicks to care much about books and writers."

I anticipate the rise of Indie bookstores—places that care about you and what you are reading, and can even offer recommendations. I go into chain stores and love the smell, but I'm increasingly discouraged by employee book-drones who clearly haven't read a book since grade school. ("How do you even work here?" "I know how to brew espresso; I don't need to read.") I'm envisioning a place like a literature version of the record store in John Cusack's High Fidelity…and I've been in stores just like that. Hopefully stores can figure out how to work with Indie authors and not see them as a mere revenue source to be exploited. That will mean not screwing over writers with terrible consignment terms and demands for wholesale pricing agreements lower than market norms (which drives up prices, destabilizes the market, and turns readers and writers away) … it will also mean Indie retailers ought to find a familiarity with any work they agree to carry and not pretend to be mini-me versions of those soulless bookstore giants in an effort to make a couple bucks.

If larger stores (and smaller ones, too,) don't figure out how to connect with real people again they fall the way Family Christian Stores and Borders have done. People can cry about the decline of brick and mortar, *or* stores can try and retain their relevance.

Tristam doesn't believe that Amazon killed the retail giants—rather, they shot themselves in the foot. The internet does a much better job at being a nameless, faceless conglomerate whose warehouse has everything in stock at any given time—and that's where Books A Million will fail: they can't stay afloat if they try to compete while limiting their stock. It has become a Fifty Shades of Beige for lasting consumer appeal and it has poked Indies in the eye at the same time.

Maybe BAM doesn't hate indie authors—but they certainly don't want anything to do with us at this point. Until they come to terms with the fact that readers want more than what the big four publishing houses put out each year, they won't ever be able to harness the power of millions of readers and writers who are the heart of a movement.

How Do I Get my Book listed on CBD (Christian Book Distributors) or Catalogue Services?

If you don't know about CBD.com, it's basically the Amazon.com specific to explicitly Christian entertainment media and gifts—kinda like the biggest Christian bookstore you've ever been to but in an online and catalogue format (plus an online portal). CBD isn't alone; many different regions have similar services including The Good Book, Christian Supply, Autom, and many more.

If you're an Indie or self-published author of ECPA or CBA style titles you would certainly want to be available through those markets, right? So how do you get into their catalogues?

I contacted CBD. Got very little. Contacted again with several more specific questions—got very little data. Many emails later I finally tracked down some contact info, called them, and got to the bottom of what I wanted.

Their site has some misinformation (or at least some very misleading/poorly written info. While there is a statement on the CBD site which seems to state that you can get carried by their distribution system if you are self-published, their online FAQ states: "Unfortunately, we are not able to accept unsolicited product queries, proposals, or manuscripts. We simply cannot accommodate the numerous requests we receive and we do not review any materials sent to us; but we'd be happy to suggest other resources for assistance." (I do believe that it was *my* multitudinous communication attempts that made them post this statement which was only added after all of my pointed questions).

Through all my investigation, here's what I found: it's not impossible to get in to the CBD catalogue, but it's not easy, either. They are *very* reluctant to give any info on how you can get in. Under one page they promote "self-publishing" and ask, "want to see your book on CBD?" The link redirected to a pay-to-play manuscript hosting service. It seemed like a back door into their catalogue since I couldn't find any info on how to get in other than being published by a big, traditional CBA house. It was a dead end, though. The link focuses only on getting a publishing contract through one of those traditional houses.

In trying to discern if it was even possible to get in as an Indie I remembered that I had purchased an indie book via CBD several years ago—that Indie house had once offered me a contract (but was also a bit of an author-mill that focused on making money from author services rather than on book sales.) Armed with that knowledge I'd asked CBD for a list of publishers they purchase from... they refused to give me that saying the list was too big (that doesn't seem valid—I could literally copy and paste the entire Bible and it would go through... there may have been some confidentiality concerns on their part, though. But it's not like I'm WikiLeaks or anything.)

I scoured the internet and did find one publisher who specifically mentioned that they could get authors in to the CBD catalogue: Bookbaby, (who is otherwise a vanity press—this is maybe their one redeeming point). I called them.

Bookbaby did speculate during our phone call that the reason they handle a large volume of Christian Indie authors is that they market their ability to harness the power of christianbook.com (CBD's site).

Since CBD wouldn't give me a list from their purchasing department's book buyers, I manually searched for book publishers in their system. I looked for titles by Bookbaby, Tate, Xulon, Westbow (part of Harper Collins), Xlibris, Creation

House, Crossbooks (part of B&H), Outskirts Press, Castle Gate Press, and even Createspace. I found a very limited number of titles from each of the above.

Something they told me at Bookbaby (the polite customer service rep even went to his supervisor to get me some info,) is that the exact nature of their relationship with CBD is confidential and as such he couldn't divulge the answers to my questions. I was interested in specifically what the parameters for title selection might be, but that was something that they simply could not share. They also couldn't speak to their procedures regarding procedure, (I wanted to know if they would automatically pitch a new Christian title to CBD or if the author had to specifically request as much.)

I contacted Createspace in order to see if there was some special process to get a book in. Createspace had no info for me and so I suspect there is another avenue (some inside relationship included authors had with someone in CBD's Buying Dept.) I contacted some of the authors directly who are listed in the CBD catalogue and received no answer. As I looked more and more into it, I also began to wonder if there might be something else that factors into it such as book producer or meeting a rep at a conference. After a few weeks of emails, phone calls, and research I came to only dead ends.

To answer my title question (How do I get in CBD as an Indie) the answer really is, "You can't." The bottom line is that Indies must be published by a company that has a relationship with CBD's buyers—and you must specifically ask them to make a pitch to CBD whose buying parameters are written only on the backside of the Krusty Krab's Krabby Patty Secret Formula, so we may never know.

If you want to be carried in CBD you must specifically ask your publishers to pursue that as a distribution avenue. During negotiations for my Christian humor book, John in the John, by a traditional press my publishing rep didn't know much about it either. It sounds like the path is narrow and the parameters are murky, but at least we know that it is an option, however unlikely.

Differences Between Christian and Secular Bookstores

The more I peek behind the curtain of the publishing industry, the further this rabbit hole seems to go. A wholly different set of rules seems to apply to faith-based writers. It may be both easier and still somehow harder to place your books in stores.

Sarah Bolme writes some wise words of interest to Christian Indies on her blog, Marketing Christian Books. She ought to know something about that; she is the director of the CSPA (Christian Small Publishers Association.)

On the page I cite below she cites a couple truths that faith writers ought to keep in mind.

It is extremely difficult to get Christian bookstores to stock titles from independently published authors and small publishers. This much is obvious and the reasons are far-flung with perhaps broader reasons than in secular markets ("This topic is the most important thing Christians need to think about...oh wait, you're a *National Convention Baptist of the USA* instead of a *National Convention Baptist of America?* I think you'd better leave. And now.")

Having your book in the right distribution channels is required for a Christian bookstore to stock it. This second, lesser known truth is a big deal. A decade ago when my first book came out I kind of poo-pooed the distribution stuff because I didn't really understand it. I really only knew that you needed to be in Ingram and Baker and Taylor and that Bowker was a thing I should know about, but didn't. Here it is in a nutshell: many Christian book stores don't use Ingram or B&T. They use

Christian specific distributors. Bolme notes "Even if your book is selling like hotcakes, Christian bookstores won't stock it unless they can order it from a Christian distributor. Createspace's expanded distribution will place your book in Ingram, but not in Spring Arbor." FYI, Spring Arbor is *part* of Ingram. Being in Spring Arbor means you're in Ingram, but being in Ingram doesn't mean you're in Spring Arbor.

I don't follow many blogs closely (I more or less stumble onto things like a klutzy, brain-starved zombie meandering through a county fair's midway,) but her blog is one that's worthy of unimpeded delivery to your inbox (so is mine—so signup for both asap).

Here is a link to the article on Marketing Christian Books https://marketingchristianbooks.wordpress.com/2016/10/17/how-to-get-a-book-into-a-christian-bookstore

12 People You Will Meet if Selling Books at Comicon

As a writer of SF/F/H I try to do a lot of sales at comic conventions (and I'm not along—I don't know that I've ever been the *only* author at one). After you've been to a few cons you begin to see certain trends in the kind of people you meet as you try to pitch your books. Here's a tongue in cheek look at twelve of them.

The Grandparent – This person looks like they have no idea how/why they are here. Usually look like refugees wandering in a strange new land. They are often just being supportive for a congoer they love and when they see you they might light up. "Oh! Books! Yes, I'd like something normal, please." **Will they buy a book?** Could go either way, depends on your pitch.

The Overly Serious Cosplayer – You'd dang-well better know who they're dressed up as if you choose to engage him/her in conversation. You can always tell regular cosplayers from the Overly-Serious variety by that glazed look in their eye... they're not sure if they're at a convention in real life or if the plot of the hero they love has need of something at this strange gathering. This is why method actors shouldn't do drugs—this is basically the end result. They are superior to you in every way and can't believe you don't love X as much as they love X. In fact, why are you even here—go home and watch X right now? **Will they buy a book?** No. It's not going to fit with their super-authentic costume (even though they don't see a problem with the Adidas backpack slung over one shoulder.) Pro tip. Never talk to a Deadpool cosplayer. Ever. Trust me. (You're also taking heavy chances with anyone dressed as Jared Leto's Joker).

Your New Fangirl/Fanboy – you don't know if they've somehow heard of you before or if something in your pitch connected with them, but they are *really* into what you're selling. "Are you married? I mean, I see your wedding ring, but is it serious? …ok, then would you consider adopting me?" You'll probably see this person a lot throughout the day/weekend. They may or may not stick it out and start your new online fan club after the event is over, but until then they are basically Madmartigan dosed by pixie love dust and you are his/her "sun and moon and starlit sky—without your book I dwell in darkness! I love you." "Excuse me. Wut?" "I meant I love ramen… um. I've got to go. See you in two minutes. I'll miss you." **Will they buy a book?** If they have any actual money they probably will. If you accept payment in hugs, then definitely.

Other Vendors – don't assume that they will buy it. They are probably talking to you in order to network or invite you to the kind of top-secret after-hours parties I never get invited to. Lucky you. Only pitch them if they ask about your books…it's just a courtesy, and you may see them again at a different event and don't want to seem like a pushy person. Chances are, if they are located nearby they have already heard your pitch and want to know *you* rather than your book. **Will they buy a book?** Often—but they may be more willing to barter for it with items from their table. "I'll gladly trade you one signed novel for that Sword of William Wallace autographed by Stan Lee."

Really Bad Genderbender – I'm not sure I'm comfortable with Sexy-Overweight-HarleyQuinn-with-a-5'oclock-shadow. He/she isn't always comfortable with it either and might refuse to make eye contact with people. If he/she does make eye contact, prepare for a long, cold stare of death as they rush up to tell you "cosplay is not consent, you pervert!" or "stop judging me you arrogant cis-male!" You didn't have to say a word… somehow, they just knew all about you with a spider-sense about as reliable as a frat-boy's gay-dar. **Will they buy a book?** Not even after you listen to their unsolicited political rant about gender equalities.

Blind Bartimaeus – This person knows the deal and refuses to make eye contact with anyone at booths as if they were circus carnies. They understand how it works: they have money and you want it. Often discriminating, they are usually at a con's merch area for something specific... if you saw them buy items at a different table, it might indicate their interests and open a door—*if* you can get them to look at you. **Will they buy a book?** Maybe. I settle for just getting their attention and an opportunity to pitch it.

Ernie the Klepto – while you are pitching your novel and convincing him to buy he says something like, "It sounds really interesting," and then walks off with it. If you manage to stop him he'll respond with, "Oh, I thought you were giving these away for free." **Will they buy a book?** Probably not...turns out he wasn't *that* interesting.

Empty Promise Girl – she's able to convince you of her love as easily as a boy at the Junior prom post-party. It's just as real too... and just like Brock, the all-state running-back, you'll never see her again after she leaves. "This book sounds amazing! I'm *definitely* coming back to buy this... I've just got a thing, first." **Will they buy a book?** No. You may spot her later walking on the far side of the aisle, trying not to look at you. She knows what she did. (And by this point you'd probably *give* her a book just to relive your hope that it would get read.)

The Reporter – They may be writing for a blog, a paper, or (most likely) their diary but they want to know every detail of why you are here, how much you make, where you live, your booth cost, where you ate lunch, if they can get a photo—preferably with no hat and looking forward, like at the DMV, say for a fake ID. "Identity Theft? Hahaha, wut? Noooooooo... I've got to go k bye." **Will they buy a book?** Maybe, but you've got to connect it to something they already like.

The Sweaty Perv – Often found wearing "Free Hugs" shirts and smelling like BO (perhaps thinly veiled under a glistening sheen of too-much Axe body-spray.) They will stare at your boobs/biceps or butt/junk during your book pitch and probably won't listen. These are not limited to just gross boys—there are plenty of women, too. Pro tip: use a buffer to keep a barrier to prevent unwanted conduct. "I know they're free… but I have a medical condition." Some of these folks need to know that "Cosplay is not consent." **Will they buy a book?** If they are a greasy and gross boy—no. If it's a "bad grandma" type she might just be happy to have had a conversation and buy it anyway. Side note: if it's an anime-heavy convention, *No* is always the correct answer to anything involving "tentacle monsters." Trust me.

The Collector – he or she is usually here for one of two things: 1. to meet industry celebrities and acquire an autograph or photo or 2. get free stuff from those tables that lure people over with salt water taffy or free pencils. **Will they buy a book?** Maybe—although they might initially be confused at the concept of purchasing, so be gentle… they are usually easier to sell to if you can convince them that you will be the next big author. "I met AUTHOR X at comicon back when they were a nobody!"

The Actual Customer – These are difficult to find. They might look like a normy in the sea of weird that can often be a con… they might also look exactly like numbers 1-11, so you've just got to pitch everyone: cast a broad net and hope for the best.

It might go more like this: You, to Really Bad Genderbender: "Hey! I, uh, really like your Sailor Moon with a beard thing." Him/her: "Oh thank God for an adult to talk to—I'm here doing this for my daughter who's a huge Sailor Jupiter fan… hey, did you write these? They look interesting."

Hopefully you get the point: pitch everyone, and try to do it well. Have some humor about it. I don't think that it's just because I'm a sci-fi/fantasy author that I enjoy selling at comicons. The people there are fun and there's never a dull moment or a more immersive place to engage with genre fiction fans. Just make sure you attend them prepared and have taken every opportunity to be your best *before* you commit money for booth or vendor fees.

Taking Credit Cards (Square and PayPal)

The future is now… except for some of the older crowd. Many people, even in the less technologically proficient crowd enjoy the ease of credit cards. Every day we become more of a cashless society. If you are at a book festival, signing, or author talk and don't have the opportunity to process credit card transactions, you are limiting the number of books you can sell.

In the past, taking credit cards meant having merchant accounts, paying large fees, processing minimums, bulky equipment, and a lot of tracking and hassle that made it too inconvenient for authors to deal with. Nowadays it's simple. Even large segments of the "technophobic" crowd are at least passingly familiar with how to use online banking and run an iPad or android tablet. Luckily, that's all that is required.

As a general rule of thumb, PayPal has lagged behind Square and other physical methods of taking payments, though it is still the standard for online purchases made person to person and for eBay transactions. PayPal is owned by eBay (or at least a member of the same circle of companies) and as such it's important to remember that it operates as a financial institution but it is not a bank—that means it is not FDIC Insured, etc. They do take credit cards, but cards must be linked to accounts which can mean extra steps that make it highly inconvenient for casual shoppers who just want a quick and easy transaction (that convenience is what attracts people in the first place.)

Square is a different animal from PayPal. It was created by its designers who couldn't complete a big transaction because the seller could not accept a credit card. With this in mind, Square became a convenient way for people at swap meets, yard sales, etc. to accept credit cards. As a musician who played in a band that sold t-shirts at a merchandise booth it became an effective way to sell products to an increasingly cashless demographic.

Why you should accept credit cards:

Numbers vary, but I've heard it said that sales increase 20-25% or more when a seller accepts plastic; that number certainly helps pay for those transaction fees, most of which cost only mere pennies, and then some.

In addition to the financial motivation, there are other reasons to take cards. It legitimizes you as a business in the eyes of consumers. It levels the playing field with other vendors. It encourages impulse buying (what *you* want). It eliminates the risk of bad checks.

How Square works:

Other services are pretty similar, but I'll discuss Square since I am familiar with it. More detailed info can be found at https://squareup.com.

Signup for a square account and link it to an existing bank account where you will receive payments at. Enter your address to get the card reader hardware mailed to you, and download the software app to your apple tablet, smartphone, android tablet, or compatible device. For simplicity, it's best if you run the app from a device that has a data service plan and have location settings turned on (as if you wanted to use a GPS program). Using the app, sign in to the account you created with Square and you can take payments immediately!

There is a slightly higher fee to type in the card account number/info (when/if you can't use the swiping device that plugs into your headphone jack) but it's a handy feature in case you lose or forget it, or the card refuses to read when swiping. The app also has a bunch of neat features. I have all of my books' prices saved so that I can easily tap each title to ring up the item; I also have my local sales tax rate saved in the settings to automatically add onto the total. If you don't use these features you can always do the math and type in the amount you are charging and ring up whatever amount is necessary. If you run all of your transactions through the software (including cash sales) it gives you a nice log to show sales amounts and numbers (with or without tax) which is nice if a vending event/location charges a percentage against your sales.

Other Alternatives:

I can't speak to ease of use or reliability of these others, but Square is not alone in the services they provide. Here are a number of other companies that provide a similar service. Alternatively, many mobile phone companies also have their own service as well.

Clover Go
iZettle (for non-United States users)
PayPal Here
Inner Fence
Spark Pay
Intuit GoPayment
Vend
Lightspeed
CardFellow
ChargePass
QuickBooks Payments
…and many more.

How to Line up Author Events at B&N/Chain Bookstores

Luckily for authors who want to get in on chain store signings, Barnes and Nobles released an article specifically listing the ways that authors can secure spots for signings and events at their locations. http://www.barnesandnobleinc.com/publishers-authors/how-to-be-considered-for-an-author-event/
While their website mentions that they often host people with a small following, that is not always the case. The above, official website basically says, "just call your local store."

There are a few things to make sure you've done *before* you make contact.

Get independent feedback on your book and make sure it feels professional (content is appealing, internal and external elements meet professional standards.)

Before you call, make sure that your book is returnable and has at least a 55% wholesale discount. (Indies can set this up with your Ingramspark account on a book by book basis—chains do not, as a general rule, work with Createspace. Avoid talking about Createspace since it is their main competitor. Because of this fact, most of my titles aren't even available on the expanded distribution channels within the Createspace author tools. As far as bookstores are concerned, *I hate Amazon.*)

Rehearse or roleplay speaking with a manager if you are nervous. Remember that writing is a form of communication; you want to represent yourself well as a professional communicator.

•Know your ISBN.
•If you have specific and relevant good reviews, use them.
•Have a press kit prepared so that you can send it at the drop of

the hat.

•Do your homework. Know who/where you are calling.

When I started securing signings, I called a random B&N and asked to speak to the CRM about a signing. The location was a store that I used to spend a lot of time in, but because of its location and area decline they rarely held author events there any longer. He *did* refer me to the largest store in his area and gave me its CRM's name. *Tip:* always ask for more information than you think you might need. The next store was able to set up a future event (partly because I name-dropped the first CRM, and partly because they immediately looked up my book on Amazon and found good reviews.) In order to have the best sales possible (which is in the store's best interest—it's not considered greedy to make this happen,) I asked two things: 1. what do you normally expect from authors and 2. what times/days seem to generate the best results for sales and/or foot traffic. Eagerness to help the store succeed is the right kind of enthusiasm to demonstrate.

The CRM might say yes, they might not, but this is the right person to talk to. He or she has the power to book whichever authors they want at a local level provided the wholesale discount and returnability are set properly. While some chains do not accept POD or independent books (Books-a-Million) Barnes and Nobles' CRMs are not tied to any rule against them. Past bad experiences, however, with unprepared writers or poorly produced books can make some of them reluctant. Sell yourself and ask how you can overcome any potential objections—some CRMs who might be opposed to an Indie author signing might be less resistant to using you at a larger "local authors" event or a "new authors" day if they have that sort of event (there are typically no more than once per year, but can draw larger crowds.)

The trick to securing a book signing is as simple as picking up a phone and calling. That's easily the biggest part. Fear and lethargy often win the day and many authors simply talk themselves out of asking.

Fear can be very real: learn to fake it if you have to, but you've got to make the call (pump some Eye of the Tiger beforehand if it helps, but pick up the phone.) If you've been rejected before call the next store. If it happens a few times, feel free to ask the event manager for feedback on your pitch and permission to call back in the future. Use smaller rejections to prepare for greater future success. Everything can be a learning experience.

A couple things to remember about setting up signings at chain bookstores:

•Approach book stores several months in advance of your targeted date.
•Be prepared to "pitch" an event manager or coordinator.
•Help spread the word through *all* media outlets (free and paid) available to you.
•Double check everything (if it's an indie store, make sure they have books for your signing!)
•Travel with a toolkit that includes pens, promo materials, etc. Mine includes pushpins, rubber bands, and duct tape—all of which have saved the day at different times.
•Pre-decide on any passages for readings.
•Be sure to send a thank-you and follow up with everyone involved.
•This list applies to smaller, independent stores as well.

Where Indie Authors Waste the Most Cash

I enjoy cooking (mainly because I enjoy eating!) At one point, I considered launching a small BBQ joint and even consulted the Small Business Association for details. "The most important thing in a new venture," the advisor told me, "is being able to limit waste." It's not any different in other businesses, either. And that's what writing is: your business.

I was sitting in the back of an after-party at a comicon with another author (cuz that's where they stick the writers... actually, we migrated there naturally,) and we were laughing about writing-related places/things that were an absolute financial suckhole—things that were a colossal failure to even make back the money paid. These were usually author services or advertising avenues. Most of our experiences were the same, and we universally agreed that dollar for dollar, we wish we'd have spent the money on editors, instead. I ran the question by the forums at a few high-traffic author sites.

Without further ado, here is a list of the top worst places to spend money for authors:

•Blog Tours & social media blitzes (twitter tours)
•Press Releases
•Writers contest entry fees at print journals
•Online Writers Courses or Classes
•Manuscript submissions services
•Multiple books on the art and craft of writing (more so if you never get around to reading them--buying them can be a form of procrastination for many)
•Subscriptions to writer's websites
•Travel for Conventions outside of writers' areas

(conventions/conferences are a great investment, but there are usually ones close enough they don't require airfare)
•Professional Video Trailers for Books
•Paid Beta Reviews
•Writing Software that went unused

Granted, this is not by any means an exhaustive list—but it includes the items that were repeatedly noted by other authors. Some items might prove profitable for some people, so this list isn't a "never use these things," kind of warning. It should, however, remind you that if you're going to pay for any of the things on the list you should certainly count the cost and understand that it might be a wasteful venture. There might be ways to achieve the same end result for free, and if you're on a tight budget, your spending dollars might be better served elsewhere.

Another comment that came up from many authors alongside those large money holes were time wasters. Spending too much time on bad promo efforts was big. Copy and pasting the same message to four-hundred Twitter feeds or Facebook groups is a huge time-suck; nobody pays attention to those posts anyway, the posts become white noise. Many of those groups are mostly full of bots and fake accounts anyway; they are incredibly cluttered (even if you get a sale after those four hours, four hours spent doing marketing correctly will pay off better in the long run. Think in terms of effectiveness and strategy.)

Where money is best spent, in my experience, is in editing and cover art. A solid cover helps open the door and pique a reader's interest. Inevitably, they will crack it open and read a couple paragraphs or click the Look Inside feature. If the first things they see are clunky sentences, boring writing, or errors, they are apt to pass on a purchase.

As I've promised to so many people, you *can DIY Indie publish your book with no cash out of pocket*. It is absolutely possible!

Most people don't have the full skillset required and everyone should try to outsource things like edits and beta reads so they get fresh eyes and perspective on a story, and depending on your connections this could be free. Some people will sprinkle in wisdom and set a budget, even a small one, and try to step up their game. If you are pooling some money to invest in your book the best expenditures you can make are 1. editing and 2. cover art... and in that order.

How Can I Change my Goodreads Cover?

Perhaps you've seen an older version of your Indie book on Goodreads with a dreaded, early edition of the cover that you wisely changed at some point (maybe due to an error on the cover, maybe you upgraded a sub-par cover with a better version, or just plain wanted to see a change.) You will have likely realized that Goodreads *does not allow cover art changes* for books in its system. It's probably the biggest fly in the ointment as far as author tools go. When you put your book into the Goodreads library it does have a warning about that restriction. You might have never noticed it, though—or someone else may have put your book into the library (perhaps a reader or fan who really wanted to shelve your book and show it off to his or her friends.)

Never fear, there *is a way* around the "no new covers" rule! You can use what's called an *alternate cover edition*. The Goodreads' help file describes the process and mentions those above reasons for alternate covers. They also talk briefly about Advanced Review Copy books and note that some users might mistakenly upload a cover from an ARC. The process for correcting is different for both instances (cover revisions and ARC entries.)

If you are updating your cover for any reason other than the current entry being an ARC cover you should manually enter the book into the Goodreads system (visit https://www.goodreads.com/book/new) and leave the ISBN fields on your new edition blank in the Description field; an ISBN can only be used once in the database. List the ISBN of the original cover edition and state that this new entry is an alternate cover edition. (You can also use the Librarian Note feature found near the top of the book edit page to attach a note to the book. This helps prevent the book from accidentally being deleted by a librarian who thinks it is an invalid entry. **Do not** use the Edition field for information about alternate cover editions.) The publication date for an alternate-cover edition should be the date the book was released with the *new cover*, not the date the book with that ISBN or ASIN was originally published

If you need to alter an ARC or galley copy, delete the ISBN number from the ARC edition. Then add a Librarian Note stating that this is the ARC cover and the ISBN number is being moved to the published edition. You can then add the ISBN number to the published edition when manually adding that new version. **Please note that this is the *only* case where an ISBN or ASIN should be removed from a published edition.**

There's usually a work-around for even the stiffest regulation. I would also recommend getting involved in a couple boards on Goodreads. It can often prove helpful to know a few folks who have Librarian status—sometimes it's the only way to fix certain issues or mistakes that we Indies sometimes make before we're proficient with a system.

Here Come the Pirates

I was selling books at my booth at a comicon and had been discussing my stories with an interested person I was pitching them to. He actually had the gall to simply tell me he would read it after he pirated it from the internet. Maybe he forgot who he was talking to in the moment, I dunno.

It kind of took me aback for a second, but we had a quick chat afterwards about ethics and piracy and how some of my stories have made more money for internet pirates than they've ever generated for me. In fact, one of my books was so blatantly stolen that it was reposted under a new author with the same summary description and a poorly edited cover with an altered title and with my name covered with a black box and new name superimposed over top of it.

In retrospect, I don't think he "had the gall" to tell me his intentions. I think I had a good enough rapport with him that he was just being honest and it kind of slipped out. When I think of books and publishing, e-piracy isn't usually the first thing that comes to mind… I always think of movies and music as being the target of pirates because our culture has told us so much about it… pretty much every video since the 1980s has had some kind of FBI warning listing the consequences for intellectual content violations and the Napster scandal of the early 2000s told us that Lars, Metallica's drummer, would personally show up at your house and beat you with a wooden shoe if you downloaded his music illegally. Nobody has really talked about books… I mean, can pirates even read?

Interestingly, Nielson's did a study on book piracy, as reported in the NYT in March 17. "E-book piracy currently costs U.S.

publishers $315 million each year in lost sales." I know this sounds benign as an Indie/self-published author… but when you look at it realistically, it means that YOU are a U.S. publisher—so this has direct bearing on you.

Here are some of Nielson's findings.

•The majority of illegal downloaders are 18 to 34 years old, educated and wealthy (the digitally savvy generation).

•Roughly 30% of illegal downloaders either obtain their content from friends via IM, email, or flash drive or from downloading from public/open torrent sites.

•Illegal downloaders acquire, on average, 13 to 16 eBooks per year—only 3 to 7 of these eBooks are acquired illegally.

•Men are more likely to pirate a book then women (66% of illegal downloaders are male).

•44% of illegal downloaders surveyed reported that they would be much less likely to illegally download eBooks if they believed it harmed the author.

What I found in my conversation was that this data is absolutely true: almost half of these illegal downloaders simply don't understand how obtaining an eBook illegally affects an author. That 44% doesn't realize that they've directly impacted the writer's bottom line. The craziest thing is the mental disconnect between the wallet and the internet: "The most common age-range of an *e-book* pirate is between 30-and 44-years-old with a yearly household income between $60,000 and $99,000." Heck, if I could make even 60k annually from my books I'd do this full time!

If you want to read someone's book and make over 30k per year, you should probably pay the man. If you really can't afford it, probably just ask him or her on the condition that you will refer all your friends and leave a stellar review online! I can't think of a time I ever turned away someone who wanted to read my stories… if you REALLY can't afford to get it, there's a better way (and it even helps the author) … ask your local library to get a copy. If it's not in their network they will purchase it!

Piracy really is a thing. The below story happened to one of my books, and it isn't even my best-selling title:

I often read through my Amazon recommendations in my email— not because I'm shopping, but I like to see how well their algorithms work in pinpointing suggestions for books I might be into. They're usually pretty spot on, so kudos there. I opened an email because my short-story/eBook, Shadows of a Superhero, was the top recommendation for me and I thought that was ironic. I scrolled down and a few books below it and found a book called Superhero X.

Maybe I should be flattered, I mused. Some guy stole a book cover that I designed and made in Photoshop—although his/her rebranding was poorly done. I clicked the ad and read the info/blurb... this was actually *my whole book*. I wrote this cover text for a version of this book at a different, popular website! I opened the "Look Inside" feature. It was a copy and pasted, blatantly thievish steal. Whoever Alexandr Shishkov is, he didn't even bother fixing the margins that he'd messed up while doing a poor format job. He also sold it for triple the price and had enrolled it in Kindle Unlimited (which means he was making 70% off each sale, or $2.10 whereas I was selling it for .99 and making about thirty cents per sale.)

Honestly, I was angrier about the poor representation and crappy formatting of the stolen and rebranded product than I was with the theft. After opening the Look Inside feature I just about lost it when someone else claimed they held the copyright... the first line says "Thank you for downloading this eBook. Thank you for your support."

Thank you Alexandr Shishkov for teaching me how to fill out copyright violation paperwork. That's something I know about now. I'd heard about things like this happening before... I guess that I always thought someone stealing my blood, sweat, and tears would try to be less overt about it.

Sellers beware. There's always a new scam right around the corner—and some of those thieves likely think that this is a victim-less crime. I never really thought something like this would happen to me... at least not until I had gotten a bigger following. Truthfully, it was quite early in my writing career, so let it be a warning—run searches on yourself with regularity and expect that someone is always trying to rip you off.

Protecting Yourself from Legitimate Publishers

I feel like I might be late to the show by rebroadcasting some great, recent advice on the business side of the writing world. Stumbling onto his article was my first introduction to Chuck Wendig… and I'm now a fan. He offers some great advice in his blog post: <u>A Hot Steaming Sack Of Business Advice For Writers</u>. (He writes an awful lot like me—or maybe just how I aspire to be—and I thoroughly enjoyed his uncouth cuppa advice over at terribleminds.com).

I'd recommend you go to his site and read it for yourself (budget a little time—it's a long article), but wanted to highlight a couple key points which parrot what I've been saying for a long while. Perhaps his best advice is his thoughts on marketing:

> You   Are   Not   A   Marketing   Plan
> Some publishers want you to be. Or they claim you should be. But you're not. What I mean is this: I think when social media became such a big damn deal that some people inside publishing were quietly cheering — first, because it genuinely provides a new axis of access for book discovery, but second because the writer can shoulder the burden…

> A publisher who pretends you're their only marketing plan is a publisher who isn't spending money on your book, and your book will succeed more by happenstance and luck than by any engineered effort on their part. (Also, if they're acting like you're their marketing plan, might I suggest billing them for marketing hours, because that's very seriously supposed to be their job, part and parcel of the relationship you enter by signing with a publisher…

It's best to demand that they actually have some plan in place, and ask to see that plan. You can even ask before you sign the contract. And you should. if you're the only one drumming up those opportunities and the publisher is simply cheering you on: they're not doing their job, because you're doing it.

Don't work for free. Rarely worth it. Exposure is something hikers die from, and authors can die from it, too. If you do work for free, know the concrete benefits, and be sure to control the work — as I am wont to say, if you're going to be exposed, then goddamnit, expose yourself. Not like that. Put your pants back on.

"What you do has value, so claim value for what you do."

I work pretty dang hard doing the things that a publisher ought to do at times... which was my expectation as an Indie author. I recognize that a publisher will want to see a strong platform and so I am pursuing that—but the trick is not to devalue yourself in the process. Remember, as an Indie author you invested in this story you wrote—it's a piece of your heart. Don't give it away as if it has no meaning or value. I'm not saying never give your story away... I'm saying *you are valuable and should remember your worth, however you decide to market yourself.*

Everyone is looking for the easy way. You shouldn't be the only one doing any work just so you can wear a publisher's brand name label.

Blog With Purpose

I almost titled this the Purpose Driven Blog, but I hear Rick Warren's lawyers are pretty good. I pulled some good advice from an interesting blog post titled Using a Blog to Reach Your Readers: http://cayceberryman.com/using-a-blog-to-reach-your-readers/

I was intrigued by the author's comparison of a blog to a restaurant. "Let the sign guide them" is a good idea. Someone who's in the mood for a cheeseburger doesn't usually walk into a sushi joint—if they do, you should expect they'll leave if they don't have something to hook them immediately.

Berryman talks about incentive and notes how bloggers don't want to write things if nobody is ever going to see it, hence the need to provide something that meets a need or interest of the blog's readership:

> If your book has vampires, I bet you can snag a list of 10 must-see vampire movies before you read my book. I bet, if you write about zombies, you can create a zombie-hunting toolkit (with a list, not physical stuff). If your fantasy world is new and complex, you can create a guide to navigating a world with rogue spirits or even something very narrow like 20 secrets a telepath won't tell you.
>
> These things are customizable, of course, but anyone interested in your story genre/theme will also be interested in the incentive. I'd click on the last one for sure. I don't need it, but if you're writing fantasy, there are few things you can offer a reader that they *need*. Give them something fun. Something they want. But don't give them

something like 10 ways to die in a bathtub if your story is about a man who falls off a plane and into another dimension or something.

You can research incentives for your particular niche and see what others offer. Make sure you customize any idea to fit your needs, though. You can always offer an incentive. But after you do that, make sure you already have posts for them to go to. Keep your blog consistent and focused.

Even if you start out with a great niche and are focused on your topic with laser vision and unique insight, it's easy to stray. Passion can wane and it's easy to drift off topic or get sidetracked with other interests (I can't tell you how many publishing professionals and authors I've watched damage their platform with post-presidential rant after rant as if they intended to rebrand themselves as political bloggers.) Straying too far from your purpose can be worse than making your audience apathetic: it can alienate segments of your platform.

Berryman's well-rounded post about blogging is one I'd recommend people read. We can all find something (as I did) to take away. Honestly, I need to get better at keeping focused but always felt like giveaways and the like were hokey gimmicks. Maybe they are, sometimes… or maybe I just haven't seen anything that really excited me enough to sign up or follow a blog (at least by way of a tangible incentive outside of the blog content… but those two or three times that I HAVE done that resonated with me.) Don't just blog because you have to put out new content each week—make each post count.

Many Authors Pay Sales Tax Twice – Don't!

Not every part of being an author means I get to live in a fantasy land full of adventure. Many parts are boring. If ever there's an enemy to creativity it's a tax form. But to have success as an author you're going to need to be familiar with taxes.

My epic tax journey begins on the phone with a tree nursery. I jointly own a very small Christmas tree farm that plants less than 2 acres of seedlings every year; we've been doing that for a few years now so the nursery asks us why we haven't filed a form so we can purchase our seedlings without paying sales tax—which is something you can do when you produce a product for resale. It's why farmers get tax exemptions for gas on field equipment, parts, etc. My grandparents on both sides farmed—it's a wonder I didn't think of it before.

Fast forward a month and I'm purchasing about $400 worth of books (my wholesale cost) for an event when I have the thought, "shouldn't this be tax exempt the same as buying seedlings?" Createspace did not have a ready answer for me and so I had to purchase those books and pay sales tax. The event coordinators required me to have all my tax document ducks in a row and so I began ferreting out the info—especially when they announced a state tax collector would be on hand to demand tax payment at the end of the three-day convention. I felt like I was in Biblical Rome… I assumed failure to prepare tax documents resulted in crucifixion.

Createspace did tell me that they have a process, but it's up to me to know the details since it varies from state to state. Here's their response:

Greetings from CreateSpace.

We do not collect sales taxes in all states for retail orders. For states where we do collect sales taxes, your purchase is subject to sales tax unless it is specifically exempt.

If you are a reseller making tax exempt wholesale orders, please submit the appropriate Uniform Sales and Use Tax Certificate and Reseller Certificate to the email, address, or fax number below:

Email: info@createspace.com, Attn: CreateSpace Direct Reseller
Fax: (206) 922-5928, Attn: CreateSpace Direct Reseller
Shipping Address:
CreateSpace
Attn: Customer Service
4900 LaCross Road
North Charleston, SC 29406

Please allow one week for form processing. For additional information, please refer to the form instructions or your state's Department of Revenue.

If you're like me, your eyes gloss over when you read things like the above. Luckily, I'd already been forced to get those above-mentioned forms on threat of crucifixion. The form I needed in Minnesota is ST3 which was the same one I needed for my Christmas tree seedlings. It was actually easy to fill out once I had the other info like my sales/use number, etc. It's only about a page and flows like a W9 or W2.

A nice lady named Dianne at the MN tax office confirmed with me that (at least in *my* state) if you produce something for resale you don't have to pay sales tax on it twice and she even told me which boxes to check on the ST3 after I explained the process of buying books and reselling them at conventions.

The fact of the matter is: you don't need to let the IRS double dip on taxes and charge you twice. The difference between being a writer and being an author is that authors plan to be read by the public—as much as it's a passion and art, it's also a business venture. Be sure to run it as such and make sure that you are not paying the same fee over and over again which will eat into your profit. Being an author shouldn't cost you more than you make.

Following are a couple of great articles to help guide you on researching your tax liability as an author: www.thebalance.com/sales-tax-facts-for-book-authors-2799901 www.thebalance.com/taxes-and-the-book-author-2799907 https://janefriedman.com/author-taxes/

Go Small and Find the *Right* Readers

Many authors don't realize the impact of going smaller. In an effort to try and reach everyone under the sun we often try and make a generic pitch that will have broad appeal. Our initial instinct is that *everyone* will love our newest book and so it ought to be pitched in such a way that everyone will find it accessible.

But that's the wrong mindset and it doesn't work. We do it naturally because our books are our babies and no parent can imagine how their child might not be everyone's cup of tea. I've met a lot of kids. Many of them are little turds who I'd love to see do a few days at military academy. There's a lot of little jerks running around whose parents praise them like they are golden gods, likewise, there are a lot of bad books. But there are also many great kids who are just a little different, maybe even a little off, but are nonetheless amazing.

Some adults would love to coach little league—others would rather tutor kids for band or theater. Kids aren't one size fits all and neither are books. When we try to make kids uniform we strip them of what makes them unique. The same goes for books—if you water down things like genre distinctions in order to give it a broader audience you will only succeed in turning *off* a larger audience with a book that *no longer fits anywhere*.

I see it all the time as a book reviewer. People know I like sci-fi and fantasy and so I get many authors trying to squish a literary fiction tale into a sci-fi mold (yes… SF is broad, but a modern romance tale about two lovers texting their feelings to each other via iPhone would've been sci-fi fifty years ago… today it is romance and not SF.) Don't make your book into something it's not.

Look for small-batch quality instead of mediocrity purchased in bulk. Two gushing five-star reviews will get you better results than fifty three-star reviews which cumulatively say "meh," about your book.

I've told a bunch of Indies this advice, "It's better to have *one or two* people who absolutely love your book and will tell everyone that they've got to read it than it is to have a hundred people who thought it was okay enough to buy. Pitch to everyone, but *find those two people*."

There are a lot of good articles about this online that give pointers on how to find and cultivate relationships with this people.

Stop watering down your book. Let it stand for what it is—even if it means there's a seemingly smaller readership. It's even okay, if you only write in a certain genre and your audience says that they dislike that genre, to stop the pitch entirely with the knowledge that you're trying to sell someone the wrong product. Don't sell a Nut Roll to someone with a known peanut allergy—focus on a better audience.

Don't advertise *broader*—advertise *better*. People will cross genre boundaries on a personal recommendation.

Why Did my Amazon Reviews Disappear?

I've written before about how crucial of a role reviews play for authors—especially on Amazon.com which is responsible for well over half of a typical author's online sales. That said, it feels like a devastating blow when a good review suddenly disappears. It happens. It happens often enough that there has been much written on the topic. That doesn't change that fact that it feels like a kick in the nuts when it happens—especially when you practically had to bleed in order to get reviews in the first place.

Tracey Cooper Posey does a pretty good job over at her blog of summarizing the history behind why Amazon enacted certain rules to keep the integrity of book reviews more or less intact (http://tracycooperposey.com/amazon-reviews-being-deleted/).
Mass deletion campaigns started in response to some major TOS violations (I remember this happening around the time of my first novel release). Info can be found online, but it came down to review mills: small companies and private contractors could be hired to post fake, positive reviews in order to make a title appear to be selling many copies and/or have rave reviews. That's a huge no-no on Amazon.

There are specific things that flag your reviews for review by the T-800s that run Amazon's Terminator algorithms. Here are four reasons why your Amazon reviews might be pulled down.

•They came from known friends and family. You're not supposed to get biased reviews and so anything obviously coming from a friend or relation will get yanked. You need those reviews, so have friends avoid mentioning a relationship.

•They all came from the same location. Amazon isn't stupid—if all of your reviews come from the same IP address, they are going to jump to conclusions and assume foul play.

•They were too vague. Generic or bland reviews are often an indicator of purchased reviews which can be bulk copied and pasted onto literally any book—they don't really sway opinion and aren't helpful to customers and so Amazon pulls them.

•They were purchased. Straight-up against the rules and unethical… water gets murky when you start asking "what do you consider 'buying' a review?" (see below for that).

Perhaps the best course of action is to ensure that you prevent having your reviews flagged by Skynet's terminator machines in the first place. Here are four tips to that effect.

1. Maintain a line of separation with readers. Authors should get an "author page" for Facebook to keep that boundary. Sometimes the Amazon death robots troll the waters of social media to see if any of your reviewers like/follow your personal profiles so that they can zap reviews and kill your hopes and dreams. (It may be part of a plan to force writers to utilize Amazon Author Central.)
2. Add a disclaimer to your reviews/make sure your reviewers do as well if they received a free copy. It helps point out when the reviews where requested and lets you note that some kind of relationship has occurred in the process of obtaining a review/putting a book in a reviewer's hands.
3. Be careful what you're linked to (understand what Amazon considers "financial compensation.") If you've purchased a gift card through your account as part of a give-away and the winner buys your book Amazon will take down any resulting reviews. They assume it was a kind of kick-back. You can't buy and send reviewers a copy of the book for the same reasons.

It has gotten tricky because Amazon sometimes takes a hard line when it comes to defining "financial compensation." If you send a copy of a physical book after a review as a thank-you those reviews sometimes come down. If you gave money to a charity to help a blind cat with mange that was featured in an Alanis Morisette television commercial and your reviewer once bought an Alanis album, it might come down. Yes. Sometimes they can be *that draconian.*

4. Backup your more authoritative reviews (from well-known reviewers/services, etc.) under the editorial review section of your author central profile. This doesn't necessarily help with your star/review rating but it preserves good reviews and puts them front and center for browsing customers.

Also, for your peace of mind it might be best to seek reviews as ardently as possible but never read them closely. If you've ever gotten a 1 or 2 star review you know what I'm talking about. From what I've gathered online, it may also be wise not to poke a sleeping bear. I've read stories from authors who sat through hours with Amazon customer service only to receive threats of having their books banned and dropped from the site for questioning Amazon's authority... kinda like giving an M4 and a license to kill to a power-mad mall-cop. I've had my own issues with Amazon customer service and would recommend seeking new reviews rather than chasing down old ones that the Internet demons dragged away in the middle of the night—after all, your next biggest fan is right around the corner.

10 Ways People Can Help Authors Succeed

Friends and family take note! This is how you help Indie authors succeed. If you're a writer and anyone has ever asked how they can best help you (and they're not an industry professional,) share this list with them!

1. Write a review! (Any place online is good, but Amazon, Goodreads, BN, Smashwords--in that order of importance--are best because of the way they run online algorithms.)
2. Offer words of support. (It's hard. Writers need to know someone out there is even reading them.)
3. Suggest their book to a book club.
4. Follow his or her blog. (hint hint. There's a little "follow" button hiding on my blog's page; go give it a visit.)
5. Add their book(s) on Goodreads and share with friends.
6. Follow them on social media. (Even better, interact with them on a variety of platforms!)
7. Talk about their book with friends. (Word of mouth is the most powerful promotional tool there is.)
8. Give their books away as gifts. (If you have a personal connection to the author you could probably have copies personalized as gifts.)
9. Suggest your local library carry the book. (If the writer open to it, ask your librarian to host a book event with the author.)
10. Buy their book! (If you bought it online and leave a review it will have a "Verified review" tag which carries more credibility than unverified ones.)

35 Tips to Help Jumpstart Your Platform and Sales

1) Brand your Facebook cover photo. Include images of any awards you may have won. According to BookBub 69% of readers use Facebook to find information about their favorite author and 88% follow their favorite author on Facebook.

2) Create a discussion on Quora. Get involved. Ask questions, engage users, don't make it all about pitching your book. Use keywords in your post title and content to increase promotional returns.

3) Have experience with public speaking? Give a talk at an event. Pitch your subject to a writers' conference, such as The Great American Book Festival or other local events.

4) Start a podcast or reach out to see if you can participate on someone else's program. The more exposure, the better. Take every opportunity to reach out to others who might benefit from your expertise.

5) Submit your book as an award contender. According to BookBub, including an author's awards in their blurbs increases clicks an average of 6.7%. Try for established and reputable award programs.

6) Comment on relevant threads in Facebook groups or on other people's threads to help build your reputation as an expert.

7) Write an in-depth blog post on a topic related to or covered in your book, then reference and link to your book within the post as well as at the end as part of your bio.

8) Contribute advice and ideas to a LinkedIn group. Make sure your profile includes a link where people can purchase your book.

9) Write a press release for PRWeb. It's a great way to get some backlinks to your site and it may even generate some press interest!

10) Use discussion forums on your book's topic including places like yahoo answers. Doing this will get you in front of people who want to know what you know. Make sure you provide a link to your author page.

11) Register as a resource for the media to use in interviews and programming at Help a Reporter Out's website: https://www.helpareporter.com/ It can help you be seen as an expert in your field.

12) Become active on HubPages and publish relevant content that will establish you as an expert in your field while providing greater exposure for you and your book. Be sure to include a link to your site.

13) Post free content or excerpts from your book on Scribd. (You may also sell your book on this site.)

14) Create short presentations about topics related to your book and put them on SlideShare and similar services.

15) Share your knowledge. Have you learned a special technique for promoting your book? Offer an article for submission with Author Pub.

16) Offer speaking topics at local schools. Teachers will appreciate the break and students will be thrilled to meet an author in person. Whenever possible, tie this in to the subject or theme of your book.

17) Make a series of videos for YouTube related to your book content. With nonfiction books, you can include a series of how-to

videos. For fiction books, you can do this by including thematic topics.

18) Be smart with time and pre-schedule social media content. Doing social media marketing doesn't mean spending all day online. Use tools like Buffer, TweetDeck, or Hootsuite to schedule your day's or week's social media content in advance. This will free up your time for writing and other marketing efforts. WordPress also allows scheduling of blogs, as do many platforms.

19) Run a fan art contest. Get fans to upload their designs of one of your characters or a scene from your book on your blog or Facebook page — or have them share it using a hashtag on Instagram or Twitter. Choose a winner to receive a prize (and then get permission to use that fan art in your marketing).

20) Run a participation contest on Facebook. Have fans share your post, comment on a post, or like a post for a chance to win a free signed copy of your book or a gift card, and cross-promote the contest on Twitter, Instagram, and any other social channel where you have a presence. You can also give away someone else's book/product in order to till new soil.

21) Make each social media post visual. Tweets with images get 150% more retweets, and Facebook posts with images account for 87% of total interactions. Instead of text-only updates, include an image photo of the book's cover or a teaser quote. This will encourage fans to click, share, or like. Tools and image libraries like Canva, Shutterstock, and iStockphoto can help.

22) Partner with other authors to run themed promotions. For example, if your publishing imprint or group of friends has three fantasy books each featuring unicorns, coordinate price promotions, themed blog posts, and social media parties. Packaging these books promotionally helps each book gain exposure across the other authors' platforms.

23) Build and manage your platform well. Here's the deal with online platforms—if you only use it to promote *your* books it is doomed to fail, fall, and help birth ancient, nameless evils. Stop destroying humanity. Use platforms properly. I've had to axe sooo many people from twitter and social media because I only ever see one thing from them, and usually several times a day: "buy my book" (with a graphic of a poorly designed cover and copy/pasted blurb which fails to connect.) Use media to *connect* to readers, not *push* your agenda; only promo your books in about 10% of posts. If you want an example of someone who's mastered this, check out https://twitter.com/BrianRathbone

24) Create an author website. Your site should be a marketing tool that serves as the hub of all your online activity, from blogging to selling books to emailing a newsletter to participating in social media. Use a platform like WordPress, Squarespace, or Wix to easily build a site for free.

25) Continue publishing new books. Nothing sells backlist like a frontlist! Continually publishing new books will help you garner a wider audience that will be interested in your other books.

26) Measure the ROI of your campaigns. Analyze your return on investment for each campaign so you know what worked and what didn't. Crunching numbers might not be as fun as writing your next masterpiece, but wasting money on campaigns that didn't work is no fun either.

27) Coordinate your marketing efforts in a single week. Bestseller lists are based on the number of units sold in a single week. Target a single list so you can optimize for its cycle. Focusing all your marketing efforts, including price promotions, social media campaigns, and emails to your mailing list in a single week can help boost your book within a preset and reasonable amount of time.

28) Run targeted social media ads. Sites like Facebook and Twitter let you target ads to a fine-tuned audience based on preferences users have expressed on each social platform. This lets you advertise to people interested in similar books or genres.

30) Submit a post to Buzzfeed. Write a clever or funny tie-in to your book. The article you write can either be entirely about your book, a "which character are you" quiz, or a listicle indirectly related. For example, a romance author might write a post on "10 Sizzling Beaches to Read Steamy Romances On" and incorporate her book into the post.

31) Write and syndicate a press release. Create an informational press release announcing your new book. Link to both the new release product page and your own website for SEO purposes. Use a free press release distribution service to syndicate your press release to news websites and blogs. See: http://mashable.com/2007/10/19/press-releases/

32) Create a permafree gateway book. For example, the first book in a series can be permafree as a gateway to the rest of your series — BookBub readers are 10x more likely to click on a book that's offered for free than a discounted book.

33) Ask local media to do a story about your journey as an author. This usually works best in advance of a new release or some special event.

34) Link giveaways or promotions to your email mailing list and utilize the signup links provided by services such as Mail Chimp. I even have an initial popup to gather addresses and let people opt-in to my mailing list for all visitors to my website. It gives a coupon code and link to all new subscribers to get a free or discounted copy of my books.

35) Always look for an open door in conversation to talk about writing. Don't be "that guys" and make everything about you and

your book, but try your hardest to be known as an author. When a friend of a friend says, "I'm thinking about writing a book," you want your contacts to instinctually respond, "You should talk to XYZ. He/she is an author." Don't overwhelm and dominate conversations, but claim the title of Author as a part of your identity and broadcast that fact in an organic manner.

How to Do a Book Review

This is a pretty subjective topic, but it is an important one. Reviews are so important to an author that they can literally keep a potential bestseller from ever being discovered or becoming successful (especially in the early stages.)

The way most people leave a review is usually based on an internal metric that readers, authors, and reviewers don't really understand. It's either feelings-based or else it comes off a very harsh rubric (did it have any stray typos, maybe a minor format error somewhere or I didn't quite like a minor plot thing? ...sounds like a 2 or 3-star rating to me! [sarc.]) I've looked at some reviewers who have NEVER given a 5-star review and say, "I'll leave one when I find the perfect book." That's garbage, and honestly, those people shouldn't leave reviews. Their metric is wrong and any 4s left should be 5s and so on.

The review system is not meant to punish authors for minor rough spots in their story—it is meant to encourage creativity and buy-in from fellow readers.

I recently dropped off a friend for a driving exam. In *that* exam, the tester starts you with a perfect score and every time you don't score a perfect on some task you lose points until you fail and they end the test, or time elapses and you get your score. That metric may work for things like driving tests, college term papers, and other grading systems, but not as an online book review. We do not look for ways to fail an author—*we want their creativity to succeed!*

I strive for polite reviews which help other writers sell books rather than choosing to leave critiques over form and craft. The rate/review sections of reseller pages are not the proper place to talk about things like author's use of grammar, etc. Reviews should talk mostly of what you liked or struggled with in the context of the story.

A person has to have a fundamental hate of an author to drop a 1 or 2-star review of a book (which you can find on the 1-star reviews atheists have left on my books after discovering my day job is youth work through a Christian organization). People ought to remember that an Amazon/B&N page, etc. is essentially a storefront. I wouldn't approve of painting graffiti on someone's brick and mortar store (even if I didn't like the owners,) and I don't think it an appropriate response for online one either. I look for every reason to leave 5-star reviews rather than looking for reasons to chip away at a high review for some failure to achieve perfection. So, few books realistically hit universal standards of perfection, but that doesn't mean they aren't still perfect in their own way.

For me, 5 stars are deserved if there is something a person would enjoy about a book (and I understand that's subjective) ... I realize that reviews and ratings are a sales tool. Even if I didn't particularly care for content, if it's well done and would please its *target market*, it deserves 5 stars. You may disagree with my opinion, but remember that review boards are not academic institutions—they're forums to rate enjoyability. Seriously...50 Shades of Gray is awful in every respect, as is many other highly acclaimed or best-selling stories. But we consume the things we enjoy, not things that are perfect in craft. There's a reason *millions* of people ingest fast-food garbage meals instead of scientifically crafted protein cubes and nutrition wafers. We are consumers and we go after what we like and enjoy rather than what is perfect or best.

Really the only reason to leave 1 or 2-star reviews is if the product was grossly misrepresented (maybe a book was supposed to be about what is wrong with our political system and capitol hill… it was billed as a political expose which begins with great observations and facts over three chapters before veering off into a digression about how the reason for all these problems is humanity's infiltration by a race of lizard people in disguise. That book is totally fine as long as the reader is not tricked into its purchase and the content description was honest).

I'd back up my opinion by telling to visit my review profile on Amazon and see how it's almost all 5-star review. If you want an author to keep working at his or her craft and keep shooting for quality, then leave them 5 stars. Helping writers succeed assures you that they will keep striving for higher levels of craft (and maybe someday even hit that high mark of universal perfection.)

Reviews: The Lifeblood of Indie Authors

I read a blog entry from an author named Mary Ellen Bramwell who is signed to one of the same publishers as I am. (https://maryellenbramwell.com) She brings up a good point about our current generation's shopping habits. We live and die by reviews. Look at the rise of whole companies like Yelp that have made reviews their business.

She tells a brief experience about a wonderful moment she had at a store. The manager suggested she leave a positive online review. Human nature kicked in (apathy, laziness, whatever...) and she held off.

"Everywhere we turn these days we are asked for feedback – from our doctors, grocery stores, online merchants, mechanics, gas stations, and so on. We are inundated with requests for our thoughts," Bramwell mentions.

It's so true... everyone wants a little more from you than you give at face value. If you've ever bought a cell phone, or booked a hotel over the phone, or purchased insurance you get many follow-up contacts asking you to rate/review/provide feedback—when sometimes we just want the stupid thing we went to purchase and want to avoid the hassle!

I understand that frustration. I really do. But it's different for authors and very small businesses such as artisan coffee shops or specialty stores like antique dealers. We don't have big backing. The single greatest thing you can do to help an author that *you do not hate* is to leave a great review (even a generic 1-word 5-star review is better than nothing.) For so many of us, a review is truly the next breath of air we take.

When I used to do lots of signings for my first fantasy novel (back before Amazon's review system was much of a thing) I used to tell people this: "If you like it please tell everyone. If you hate it, tell no one."

Amazon uses different metrics to decide how the rate and rank books. If you want your book to appear higher in the rankings (be shown earlier in searches, which yields more sales,) then you need more reviews. There are many myths and schools of thought that getting more reviews means authors get extra tools. One myth claims that after 25 reviews a book unlocks the "also bought" and the "you might like" suggestive list. It goes on to say that at 50 reviews you can get spotlighted for promo positions in the Amazon newsletter.

There is no magic or set math to getting access to these tools. While reviews factor into your ranking (which helps boost sales) apparently added features like book spotlights and promos are based upon a combination of sales and ranking and comparisons to other titles. Authors who have achieved all of those sorts of goals claim that their organic sales had far more to do with these programs than reviews did—it's just that the reviews happened to come along for the ride and accompanied the sales that were made. (For you math and detail junkies, reports from authors who hit these marks say that 50 reviews mean real sales between 5,000 and 10,000 books (about half of one percent leave reviews on average).

Reviews don't unlock magic milestones, but they are necessary to sales. More sales mean more reviews. The circle keeps on spinning—and no sales with zero reviews often stays that way. Support the authors you like: book reviews literally cost you nothing and can mean the world to an Indie author!

What Do Those Stars Mean on Amazon?

If you take anything away from my writing about reviews, it should be to review books and leave them high marks. Granted, not every book is the best—and some truly deserve low reviews, but there seems like a lot of room in between, right?

One of the primary problems with the Amazon 1-5 star rating/review system is that it's highly subjective—but not just as a matter of opinions about writing and stories… but also about the review system itself. If you read a perfectly average book with no major problems, and you enjoyed the story line, but it's not cracking your all-time top ten novel list, it should split the uprights and be a 3-star rating, right?

Wrong. *It should be five stars.*

People tend to set up their reviews based on a system of product comparison, but that's wrong. *A 5-star review does not have to be the best book you ever read; neither does it have to be perfect* (lots of books have the occasional error in the minutia—both Indie *and* traditional). A 5-star book doesn't even have to be better than the *last* book you read. Three is not the middle, and in fact a 3-star review shows up as a "critical review" under the Amazon system… i.e. you thought the book was *bad.*

Here is what each of those star ratings mean:
5: you enjoyed this book in the way that it was meant (has the expected tropes, themes, etc.)

4: you generally liked the book but you have at least one major issue with the book *which detracted from your enjoyment* (lots of repetition in the writing, a major plot hole, far too many typos, etc.)

3: a novel you neither liked nor disliked—you didn't care if you finished it or not. You might read it if you were stuck on a desert island and this was all you had... then again, you might use it for TP instead. Because some advertisers and listing services don't allow 3-star books, consider leaving *no review out of apathy and sympathy. This review hurts an author's rating.*

2: the novel is plagued by multiple, serious issues and you want to prevent others from suffering in an attempt to read this book. There are typos on practically each page (lack of editing,) serious inconsistencies, or a glaring lack of research. There was a plot, characters, and setting, but you did not enjoy any of it.

1: a colossal failure. You hate this book so much that it keeps you up at night—*there was no plot*, this was not a story. Don't leave a 1-star review unless you truly feel the author should never write again—this is not the appropriate review to leave if you bought a romance that you thought was a "Clean Christian romance" from the cover/title but it actually turned out to be an Amish bodice ripper—that would be since the book had a story...just the wrong story.

Perhaps the best blog I've read on this topic (from which I developed some strong thoughts from) come from https://teylarachelbranton.com/reviews-what-those-stars-mean-to-authors/ (her list of Dos and Don'ts for reviewing is highly recommended).
Teyla Branton frames it in the context of a school report card: 5 stars is a B+ to A, 4 stars is a C+ to B, 3 stars is a C or C-, 2 stars is a D or D-, and 1 is an F.

On that report card theme, imagine you believe in a literal, divine creation narrative from the Judeo-Christian perspective (that God created the earth and everything on it in six days and that evolution doesn't exist.) Let's say you're also in high school and take a chapter test on Darwinian evolution. You can score 100% on the test despite having vastly different beliefs than those in a textbook. That's how this system is supposed to work: you can give 5 stars even if the book wasn't your cup of tea or disagreed with your internal worldview. However, if the book was presented as a fantasy novel but turns out to be a literary novel about a man who *thinks* he is a wizard while dealing with life inside a mental institution, it would be a 4-star novel unless it clearly states it's about a man with mental illness. "Does the book tell the story that it promised?"

Because Amazon runs with an average and because 3-star reviews actually translate as negative, this is how to interpret the 1-5 star rating system:

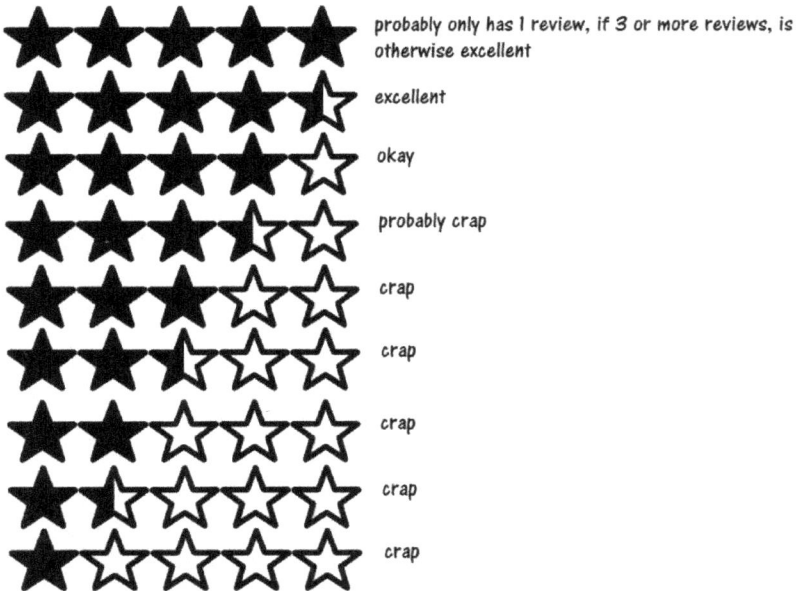

★★★★★ probably only has 1 review, if 3 or more reviews, is otherwise excellent

★★★★☆ excellent

★★★★☆ okay

★★★☆☆ probably crap

★★★☆☆ crap

★★☆☆☆ crap

★★☆☆☆ crap

★☆☆☆☆ crap

★☆☆☆☆ crap

How to leave Amazon star ratings/what Amazon's star ratings really mean

Remember—this review might be the most important thing for any given author! Handing out low reviews is perhaps the biggest kind of insult you can give any author. Remember that movie you saw in the theater—the one that you didn't hate and kinda liked, but the details and plot were a little fuzzy in your memory by day two?

That murky Hollywood hangover churned out on a daily basis by the movie industry earns them millions of dollars. Make an author feel like a million bucks today: leave a 5-star review... they probably deserve it more than you've ever even realized.

Indie Authors Might Save Our Culture

There is a school of thought out there that says nobody would publish as an Indie author if they could go traditional. The thought goes something like this: "serious writers don't do that;" Indies spend all their time doing publisher stuff so they never get to write; publishers know the market best; Indies can't make a living writing; and the big one: Traditional Publishing Creates a Far Superior Product.

While there are some truths to these myths, (yes, Indies spend an increased amount of time spent marketing—but I'd point out that I wrote 3 books this year, so it's not a rule,) some of those myths are complete fabrications. The commonly held notion that traditional publishers create better books is flat-out untrue.

Yes, many Indie books have horrendous covers (usually put out by people who don't have a clue about industry standards or know how to do things correctly—hence this book.) I would argue that content must also be a factor.

Publishing is a business and business revolves around high sales income with low overhead—product quality is only a factor if the audience demands it... and that's not always the case (exhibit A would be the steaming heap that is 50 Shades of Grey... to quote one popular industry professional, "sometimes people just want to read a dirty book." The market demanded the book and they weren't so picky that they needed their porn to be properly edited.)

The music industry is a great example of "the industry" giving us cookie-cutter, force-fed products. Listeners have had Nickelback and Nicki Minaj forced on them for so long that many people don't even know what good music is and will complain if you put in something with real substance. Compare a guy like Israel Kamakawiwo'Ole with Beyoncé—or heck, *any* modern artist. Compare the million-dollar machine turning Beyoncé albums into gold with Bob Seger or Johnny Cash. Sorry if you like Beyoncé, and I'm not saying that her songs aren't catchy, but Beyoncé plays no instruments and lives and breathes via auto tune, casting even her ability to sing in doubt. The machine does *one thing: sell albums.*

I'm not here to trash anyone, but here's the rub: commercial industries are concerned with following a formula and selling the specific brand of "stuff" that they have artificially created a market for. The music industry isn't selling music; they are selling what they want you to *think music should be*. This model actually stifles creativity and shrinks the breadth of work available to the listening public and limits the kind of stories that we see produced. A great example of independent people succeeding outside the box is found in the craft beer market. Once legal restrictions relaxed, crafters bearing intense passion exploded the industry and revitalized that fire in other beer drinkers. Specific taste became relevant again—finally becoming more important than whatever beer advertised the most or had the funniest commercial during Monday Night Football.

However, there is a relevant truth in those Indie vs Traditional myths: traditional works typically *do* have better editing and more concise language—their content has usually been thoroughly reviewed. It's not that "traditional house" stories are better; it's that they've had more professionals refine the final product—even if it's an otherwise mediocre or uninspired one.

I'm not saying traditional houses have less talent or imagination—rather that it's not necessarily better for the literature community as a whole to wholesale judge an entire community without just cause.

Many famous bands recall fondly their days playing small bars and tiny dives—some of them sneak out and play surprise shows at old hole-in-the-wall venues. In their independence, they found their voice and a greater freedom to express themselves and experiment with their craft. Some, like the tortured musician Kurt Cobain, longed for the ability to go back.

Kurt Cobain would've loved the opportunity to be successful as an independent artist. Be an Indie and be proud of it. You can always step up and go traditional later—but there is no need to step on the Indie scene if you ever do get there.

Book Awards

Self-published/Indie authors get a lot of discrimination, sometimes justly so. One of the areas they are often shut out of is the ability to win publishing awards of any significance. On the one hand, it might not seem like that big of a deal. On the other hand, studies show that "Award Winning" books sell about 7% more units than their peers, probably because of the perception of added value.

Authors need to ask themselves some questions: First question. "Is that 7% in sales honestly worth the investment?" You're going to want to strike while the iron is hot—if you won an obscure book award ten years ago, it's probably not relevant anymore. You will want to count the cost first. If it's fifty bucks to enter for an award and you sell less than a hundred books in a given year, the math doesn't work out. If you sell ten books a year and make $4-10 per book, as is the norm, you've made about $70. If that award helps you to statistically sell maybe one more book at the median $7 per book, you're up to $77. Woohoo. My point is that you've got to have a valid marketing/sales strategy if you're looking into this.

Second question. Will you actually win? You should have an editor, beta reader, or someone unafraid of hurting your feelings tell you if they think the book is award worthy. It might all be unicorn farts and rainbows you're chasing. If your book hasn't been edited, you are better off investing that money in proper editing instead of paying for an award's entry fee. Not all awards have a significant cash prize.

I also have mixed emotions in regards to awards sites like Readers Favorite and their ilk. It's not really a solid award when you pay money to secure a review and nearly all books receive the award. It's a way to quickly and easily put a shiny awards sticker on a book and gain that 7%... as an author, though, whenever I see books with their award on it I feel a little judgey inside. It's more of a marketing tool than a real award, so don't hang your hat on that peg too firmly. It may help you sell a few books at conventions, etc. but it's not especially brag-worthy—especially to people who know how their award system works. (Sigh… and I'll probably buy the stickers at some point… heck, 7% adds up.)

Anyhow, I wanted to share a list of Fifty Book Awards open to self-published authors:
http://selfpublishingadvice.org/50-book-awards

In the eventuality that this site might someday disappear, I'll list my favorites that indies ought to look into… ye olde google machine ought to help find the specific sites:

Amazon Breakthrough Author Award
Digital Book Awards
Independent Book Publishers Association – Benjamin Franklin Awards
IndieReader Discovery Awards
Kindle Book Awards
Moonbeam Children's Book Awards
National Indie Excellence Book Awards
Shelf Unbound Writing Competition for Best Self-Published Book

Why Readers Don't Know What They Like

When I'm at conventions or book signings I often ask, "What kinds of books do you like," or even "what's the best book you've read in the last year?" When it works, it can be a great tool to identify what kinds of books to connect them with. Very often they respond with cricket chirps. People don't know, and it reminded me of a conversation I had with my wife, a teacher.

I want to be upfront: I am not knocking teachers! My grandmother was a teacher, my mother is a teacher, my wife is a teacher, I've was a substitute for over a decade. In one of my wife's post-grad classes on she found some interesting info.

She and I had a conversation following her reading of Wilhelm's *Let them read trash: The power of marginalized texts* (2012) and Layne's *Igniting a passion for reading: Successful strategies for building lifetime readers* (2009). What she came away with was that "we teach children how to read, but don't teach them how to choose *what* to read."

My wife asked this: *Layne states that "teaching kids how to find a book is not really part of the curriculum" (78). He goes on to state that especially in elementary school we teach kids that they are a "yellow dot" reader and should find books in the library that are "yellow dot" books. Once students go out into libraries and book stores, they have to determine for themselves what their reading level is. In conversation with a friend of mine who is also an elementary teacher, she stated her students have color coded books that they are to read; they can have a couple books one color level above or below, but most have to be the correct color. I see so much structure, and dare I say* control, *in the primary grades that when students get into middle school they are helpless to find reading material without a support system. Are we creating children that are dependent on a teacher to test them and tell them what to read?*

Many kids in middle school flounder for a couple of years because they have no idea what they enjoy. Their options were limited in grade school (and low-level readers could be deterred away from engaging texts like Harry Potter because they were taught they couldn't handle big books,) and when they suddenly lose their guidance system they are left to "just figure it out." It's not just middle school kids that suffer—many people carry that fear of books with them into adulthood.

Add on top of this that Common Core is intrinsically opposed to teens reading fiction. (They have never shied away from their desire to force readers towards informational texts and away from fiction—in the same manner the arts have been discarded in an effort to concentrate on math and sciences).

We need to teach kids how to find stories that connects with their interests. The reason video games are popular is that the story connects with players and draws them in—our current schooling teaches them that reading is a process whereby they subject themselves to an information dump, lifting mental weights to parse the information. Have you ever tried to read through a long legal document? That's the feeling kids have when reading something that doesn't engage them. It's not as easy as telling kids "Keep reading that boring stuff... eventually you'll learn to love it!" Nobody works that way... *oh, you don't like being slapped in the face? here, let me beat you until you like it!*

We've to get better at inspiring reading. Be passionate, and invite people to read with you! It goes a long way.

10 Reasons Why Should You Attend a Writers Conference

I'm not rich by any stretch of the imagination. I don't have any hopes or dreams of becoming a 1%er. I don't like frittering my money away, but I don't want to horde it like some kind of miser either. I try to invest smartly. As someone with high ambitions for my writing endeavors I am intentional about investing in myself. To that end, I try to attend at least one writer's convention every twelve to eighteen months. I try to limit my travel expenses (I usually bank up free airline miles in order to reduce prices and find cheap hotels) but I do believe I get a great value in conferences.

Usually, I come home from the seminars with a journal full of notes—things I've learned, plans I've made, and people I've met. I don't honestly think that I can digest all of that immediately... maybe not even in a year. I try to find two or three things that I can learn and implement over the next year in my writing, platform building, networking, marketing, and beyond.

Dropping a couple hundred dollars is a strategic investment. It becomes easier to spend that on yourself when you believe in your future as a writer... understand this is not a quick fix or magic pill, but if you learn a few things at a convention or workshop and work to get better at your craft, those dollars will pay off dividends in the future.

Here are 10 things you might gain or take home from a writer's conference:

•Networking with other writers
•Meeting literary agents or publishing professionals

•You will get energized and inspired

•It can be a tax write off

•You may get opportunities to pitch agents and publishers

•Your expectations will become grounded in reality (for better or worse)

•You will gain resources (notes, handouts, books, etc.) to use forever

•You are likely to find something that was never on your radar (an underground community, a newly launching service or agency, a new outlook on some topic)

•It transitions you from a hobbyist to a professional

•You'll get updates on industry trends and how the publishing world is changing

Think of it like a strategic investment and not a vacation. Yes, you will get something out of it—but there's an element of determination involved. If you've never been to one, check with state library and writer's programs, many of them have grants available to help first time attendees get out to one.

What the Heck is NaNoWriMo

If you've been around on the internet for any amount of time as an author and read articles, forums, and other posts about writing and publishing then you've probably come across the term *NaNoWriMo*. Just like any subculture, writers have their own vocabulary and this completely made up word might confuse the uninitiated.

NaNoWriMo is a combination of words: National Novel Writing Month, which happens to be November. NaNoWriMo is a challenge to write a full novel (or 50,000 words) between November 1 and midnight of November 30. The challenge has become a big deal and there are a variety of websites and methods participants may use to track and measure progress, encourage others, provide feedback, etc.

The word count is a measurement of your rough draft—not an edited manuscript. Writers are encouraged not to make edits or changes, but rather just get the whole novel written. Everything can be fixed in the edits, later.

Much like running a marathon or even a 5k, there is no prize. It's a challenge more than a competition. Every person who makes it across the finish line is declared a winner. However, many of the websites that track participants have unique incentives and may offer prizes; some participants have gone on to have their novels picked up by literary agents or publishers.

Completing the NaNoWriMo challenge, which has been around since 1999, means you have written a book approximately 200 pages in length. Divided equally, it's about 1,700 words per day or 3 single spaced 8x10 pages with normal font sizing.

The official website for the creative challenge is at http://nanowrimo.org.

When Should I Quit My Day job?

If you saw the 2007 movie Wild Hogs starring Tim Allen, John Travolta, and Martin Lawrence you might remember a great scene in the beginning. Martin Lawrence is staring at a blank page. He's been doing this for a year, now, trying to start his novel when his wife pops in to remind him that he promised to go back to his job at "The Firm" if he hadn't completed his book after a year. Turns out The Firm is the name of a sewage pumping company.

Most people, at least for big chunks of time, are like Lawrence's character: we can stare at a blank page for a long time. The dream to become a big-time author is a great one, but when there's a mortgage to pay and kids to feed, it might not be sensible. Banks don't cash dream checks... Of course, authors aren't usually sensible people. If you ask Google when you should quit your day job you will find a sea of people advising you to quit now—many claim that the added stress of a "sink or swim" mentality will somehow propel you into the upper echelons of the publishing sphere and you'll never look back.

That's some crap advice. Those articles were written by people who swam, not who sank—those people are too busy looking for jobs to write bad advice columns. Quitting too early is how you wind up flipping burgers at age 40.

Most of the people on those first few pages of a web search who advised writers to quit their jobs list the importance of things such as "multiple streams of income" and "Lifetime Value" customers. They are the people who are writers (even though I've never heard of most of them), but sell other writers online classes, courses, workshops and programs or mentoring services. That is, they sell much more than books and spend most of their time selling writers on products that most authors I've talked to say was a complete waste of their money and time in retrospect.

I'm not speaking ill of self-investment or training courses (heck, I *love* showing others how to succeed.) Writers helping writers is great. But when hooking authors for your program becomes your primary source of income then you haven't really quit your day job to write… you just took an even more volatile day job that forces you to muddy up the Indie writing pool with murky promises about what success looks like.

I've always been a big fan of hoping to be the exception while planning to be the rule. There are always those exceptions that we hear about, and yet the rule is far more likely.

We read often about authors who made $10,000 in a month, but we rarely hear about how little they made in subsequent months. The internet is stuffed full of articles about authors who made some leap of faith and became wildly successful. Towards the bottom of so many of those articles you will find a tiny sales pitch about buying their seminar or services—that alone should be an indicator. One page, put up by a "Indie Publisher" who looks suspiciously like a vanity press claimed, "it's easy, quit your day job now and publish with us—follow these simple steps and be a huge success," or something close to that.

Quite certainly I am the unpopular voice in the room when I say, "don't do it." There is at least some truth in the earlier statements that you need multiple streams of revenue to be successful… it's just that your day job is one of them. Until you've made the proper preparations and have achieved a certain amount of sustainable success do not put all of your eggs in one basket.

It's certainly not what most people want to hear—but most people who write books also want to be told that their book is "the best thing I ever read and I couldn't put it down." *They want to be the exception rather than the rule*. Really, most don't want to hear, "I found a spelling/grammar error every third page or so, one of your supporting characters has no personality, and there's a major plot-hole or inaccuracy in chapter eight." That same, self-pleasing sentiment carries over and is why we want to hear "you can do it! Quit now!" rather than the truth: writing is actually hard work and takes a lot of planning, commitment, wisdom, and effort in order to succeed—profit margins will be razor thin for longer than you want to know.

One of the wisest pieces of advice I've received on the topic has been this. "Don't quit your day job until you can no longer adequately do both jobs well (and your writing is able to carry your financial burdens.)" I'd echo that sentiment. Until you are a proficient swimmer, don't jump into the deep end without your floaties on.

List of Helpful Websites for Further Research

Below are some links to great websites that I regularly visit as I search for help to my own problems and answers to questions that pop up as I walk my own Indie road… I honestly don't have this figured out; I'm stumbling along too and this industry changes frequently—so keep reading and stay in the loop!)

http://absolutewrite.com/

https://querytracker.net

http://www.sfwa.org/other-resources/for-authors/writer-beware/about/

http://www.theindieview.com/indie-reviewers/

https://marketingchristianbooks.wordpress.com

http://terribleminds.com

http://www.indiesunlimited.com

http://pred-ed.com/

https://www.thebookdesigner.com/carnival-of-the-indies/

http://www.creativindie.com

http://authorchristopherdschmitz.wordpress.com/

About the author:

Christopher D. Schmitz is the traditionally published and self-published author of both fiction and nonfiction. When he is not writing or working with teenagers he might be found at comic conventions as a panelist or guest. He has been featured on television, podcasts, and every other medium he can get into. He runs a blog for indie authors.

Always interested in stories, media such as comic books, movies, 80s cartoons, and books called to him at a young age—especially sci-fi and fantasy. He lives in rural Minnesota with his family where he drinks unsafe amounts of coffee. The caffeine shakes keep the cold from killing them.

Schmitz also holds a Master's Degree in Religion and freelances for local newspapers. He is available for speaking engagements, interviews, etc. via the contact form and links on his website or via social media.

Dear reader,

Thank you for reading my book. If you enjoyed it or find anything helpful within its pages won't you please take a moment to leave me a review at your favorite retailer (or on Amazon.com as a safe default)? Sharing this title with your friends on social media and requesting it via your local library will also help immensely. Discoverability is the lifeblood of success for authors and we can't continue writing without help!

I also hope you will keep tabs on me by joining my mailing list. You can get free books and other updates by signing up for that list at:

www.AuthorChristopherDSchmitz.com.

Thanks for reading and sharing!

Christopher D Schmitz

Discover Fiction Titles by Christopher D Schmitz

The Last Black Eye of Antigo Vale
Burning the God of Thunder
Piano of the Damned
Shadows of a Superhero
The TGSPGoSSP 2-Part Trilogy
Father of the Esurient Child
Dekker's Dozen: A Waxing Arbolean Moon
Dekker's Dozen: The Last Watchmen
Wolf of the Tesseract
Wolves of the Tesseract: Taking of the Prime
Wolves of the Tesseract: Through the Darque Gates of Koth
The Kakos Realm: Grinden Proselyte
The Kakos Realm: Rise of the Dragon Impervious
The Kakos Realm: Death Upon the Fields of Splendor
Anthologies No.1

Discover NonFiction Titles by Christopher D Schmitz
The Indie Author's Bible
Why Your Pastor Left
John in the John
Gospels in the John

Please Visit
http://www.authorchristopherdschmitz.com
Sign-up on the mailing list for exclusives and extras

other ways to connect with me:
Follow me on Twitter: https://twitter.com/cylonbagpiper

Follow me on Goodreads:
www.goodreads.com/author/show/129258.Christopher_Schmitz

Like/Friend me on Facebook:
https://www.facebook.com/authorchristopherdschmitz

Subscribe to my blog:
https://authorchristopherdschmitz.wordpress.com

Favorite me at Smashwords:
www.smashwords.com/profile/view/authorchristopherdschmitz

www.ingramcontent.com/pod-product-compliance
Lightning Source LLC
Chambersburg PA
CBHW060316030426
42336CB00011B/1067